by EDWARD SANDERS

Poem From Jail (1963)

Peace Eye (1966)

The Family: The Manson Group and Aftermath (1971, New Edition 1990)

Egyptian Hieroglyphics (1973)

Tales of Beatnik Glory, Volume 1 (1975)

Investigative Poetry (1976)

20,000 A.D. (1976)

Fame & Love in New York (1980)

The Z-D Generation (1981)

The Cutting Prow (1983)

Hymn to Maple Syrup & Other Poems (1985)

Thirsting for Peace in a Raging Century: Selected Poems 1961–1985 (1987)

Poems for Robin (1987)

Tales of Beatnik Glory, Volumes 1 & 2 (1990)

Hymn to the Rebel Cafe (1993)

Chekhov (1995)

EDWARD SANDERS

CHEKHOV

BLACK SPARROW PRESS   SANTA ROSA   1995

CHEKHOV. Copyright © 1995 by Edward Sanders.

ACKNOWLEDGMENTS

Thanks to the editors and publishers of the following publications where some of these poems first appeared—*City Lights Review, The Cafe Review, Poetry New York* and *Cracks of Grace.*

Black Sparrow Press books are printed on acid-free paper.

LIBRARY OF CONGRESS CATALOGING-IN-PUBLICATION DATA

Sanders, Ed, 1939–
    Chekhov / Edward Sanders.
        p.   cm.
    Biography in verse.
    Includes bibliographical references
    ISBN 0-87685-965-1 (paper). — ISBN 0-87685-966-X (cloth trade). —
    ISBN 0-87685-967-8 (signed cloth)
    1. Chekhov, Anton Pavlovich, 1860–1904—Biography—Poetry. 2. Authors,
Russian—19th century—Biography—Poetry. 3. Russia—Intellectual life—19th
century—Poetry. I. Title.
PS3569.A49C48   1995
891.72'3—dc20
[B]   95-11802
                                                                  CIP

B
C 4165

Contents

Appendices 227

Chekhov

1

The Phantom from Taganrog

Who was this man
          called Chekhov
                 in the time-mist

Who was this very energetic guy
from a little grain-port
           on the Sea of Azov?

We glimpse him
         in his stories and plays,
         in the 4,000 letters that survived

         and in the words of Gorky,
         Bunin, Suvorin, his sister Maria,
         his brothers Mikhail and Alexander
                  and a few hundred others

The life of a genius
can swerve for 10,000 pages
& yet you're looking at sand

It's not clear what he was
except a writer and survivor
         who lived his productive years
                 to the constant throb
             of the TB doom-drum

         who told his tales
            wrote his plays
        built schools and clinics
            tended the rubleless sick

His life as complicated
        as any genius
                with a racing metabolism
and the ever quick'ning throb
                  of the TB drums

This phantom from Taganrog
whom we call out to
        100 years down
                into the mist

2

Chant to Russia in the Time-Mist

Holy Russia in the Time-Mist
We enter your Time-Tracks
in your complexities
        and try to forgive
             the way you harmed
                for so many centuries
                    your bent-down workers and farmers

Try to forgive
        the anti-Semitism
                and hungers for Orthodoxy

the centuries of total censorship
        your tsar-class's ceaseless
                thirst for control and bondage.

Your ancient Orthodox eyes affixed
                to the ports of the south
and the jewels of Korea, Japan and China
        to the East

Holy Russia in the Time-Mist
for whom Chekhov felt such obvious love—

for the land and its people,
        its music and writing
                the beauty of its vastness

Huge and Holy Russia in the Time-Mist

    we can't help heeding the clank of it—
    a cruel and clicking clank—
    the grind of Tsar and Church
    the grind of border-bashing
    the grind of saintly and mean-souled peasants,
    of exile, Siberia,
        white gloves and pain,
            prisoners shackled to wheelbarrows
    grinding and heaving in the Time-Mist

    and the grinding and seething too,
        brilliant and soon all-seething

        of Marx, of Lenin,
            of strikes and steely stridor,
    & the score-settling rappels of rev

3

Tsar, Church, Slavery, Absolute Power

Tsar comes from
    the Latin word Caesar
        and then Kaisar

The tsar's official title was
        Emperor & Autocrat
        Imperator i Samovlastityel

            *

15

In the old Slavonic bible
the Greek word βασιλεύς for king
is translated "tsar"
As a title it was first used by
        Slavonic folk in the Balkan peninsula
and was used by medieval Bulgarian kings
was assumed by Muscovite princes who shook
free from the Mongols
The "other" tsars over time were stomped down by
the tsars of Moscow

                        *

Modern tsars acquired their title from
Ivan IV — Ivan the Terrible
                whose jutting, bearded jaw
                        we know from
                                the Eisenstein movie

Ivan suffered from child abuse
                and took over the gov't at 14
He crowned himself tsar in 1547
                and ruled for 37 years
setting the Russian tsar-tone of
                Absolutism and Terror,
feeding his first set of enemies—
        those who had abused him—
                to hungry dogs

He suffered from paranoid fury-fits
his brain a Total Fear Zone
        analyzing slights and conspiracies

He once destroyed a large city
        and everything for a
                100 miles around
                fearing its leaders were a-plotting

He set the game for future tsars
                with his vast personal energy
his photo memory

16

his Absolute Power
His "Ego Deus Sum"

*

The Peasants

Serfdom began in the 16th century
and was consecrated in law in 1609

Sometimes it arose from conquest
Sometimes the serfs
            entered slavery "voluntarily"
                        when times were harsh
The serfs became the slaves
            sometimes on State land
            sometimes on the estates of "nobility"
            sometimes on Church lands

They were chained to their plots to
            drudge at the masters' whims

and to farm open field strips
            organized in village communes

There was every sort of cruelty
            in the cage of their masters' caprice

The serfs were kept illiterate,
        prone to rumor from isolation
            slaves of the plow
                    and game-planned

by the mooch class
        to mumble and bow

*

The tsar's absolutism
>depended on the support of
>landowners
and he therefore
>tolerated the grim exploitation
>>of the peasants

*

The Church

The Greek Orthodox Church broke away from
the Roman Church in 1054

There was the Byzantine concept of the
absolute ruler, inspired by God,
>for whom the Church with its divine authority
>was a belfry, support unit, battle-soother
>>and keeper of the ritual

When Constantinople was conquered by the Turks,
the church in Moscow claimed to be the protector of
all Orthodox Christians.

Two Romes have passed, so went the adage,
>& Moscow was the "Third Rome."

4

A Revolution in France

In France as in Russia,
the "nobility"
a clergy that believed in an Iron Jesus
and a right wing military

ran things with iron gloves

and the peasants
        were impoverished
                by feudalistic filth-rules

yet monarchy was known
        to be defeatable
as the recent American example had shown

and all the Enlightenment
the struggles of Diderot
philosophers and bards
hundreds of thousands
of leaflets
        and jail terms

for at least a hundred years
was ready to prevail

                        *

The nobility summoned the States-General
(which hadn't met since 1614)

        hoping to control
                the rappel of rev

The States-General was the seldom-used
representative body
of the French monarchy—

It had three parts:
the 1st Estate (clergy); 2nd Estate (nobility)
and 3rd Estate ("commoners")

By June of the year of rev
the "commoners" had forced the creation
of a true National Assembly

        Then, in four beautiful months:

• The Fall of the Bastille
• Abolition of Feudalism
• Declaration of the Rights of Man

Next were Experiments
     in various types of
          governing

After all, it was Something New
but there were too many tough guys
         wanting to be Dictator

aping the essence
    of what their philosophies
         had rejected

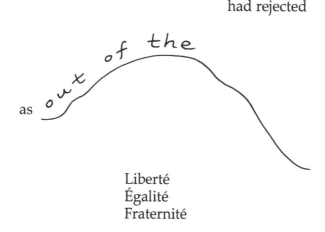

as out of the

    Liberté
    Égalité
    Fraternité

    mound

      sprang the dragons
         of death-dust

*

But "Carpe Diem" had occurred
and no right wing droolers
were going to take back
    the freedoms of '79

*

The tyrannies of Europe
           the leeching complexes of nobility
The royalist armies
           banded together
                     to war the

French Revolution

✳

The Paris Commune
(1792–93)

Political power was grabbed
by the group known as the Girondins
in late '92

The Revolutionary Convention
           formally abolished the monarchy
                     on 9-21-'92

and then in January, '93 Louis XVI was beheaded

and war declared against
           Britain, Holland, Spain

✳

Imperial
Europe was like
a microscopic
slide
    of pond water:

Tyrannies ever striving
to shove other
tyrannies out of
           the way.

And so not only did they band together
to kill the rev

they thought they might as well
scheme to
          eat French land

so that the Austrian Minister
could write that "the
return of peace ... will be a benefit
which France
          will have to purchase
                    by the sacrifice of the province
we shall have conquered."

                              *

The Committee of Public Safety

The Girondins
          failed at war
                    in the spring of '93

and the French National Convention
set up a
          Committee of Public Safety

to be
          the Executive Branch
                    throughout France

                              *

Then the Jacobins
took power in the spring o' '93
and executed the Girondins
                    on Halloween '93

                              *

Robespierre
(Nov '93–July '94)

For nine months the Jacobins
vied to set up a system
                                    of rule
based on "absolutist aspects"
of Rousseau's *Contrat Social*

Robespierre saw himself
                        as the emanation of the
                                                "General Will"
in a Rousseau-inspired gov't

but sank in the hell of serial murder
as he used *The Committee of Public Safety*
                                                to settle scores

with head-chops aplenty—
2600 were guillotined in Paris alone
                        including Danton and Hébert

Then Robespierre himself
was head-clipped
            and the Jacobin Club closed

death-dust to death-dust

✳

The Directory
('95–'99)

An entity called The Directory
ran France four years
after the Jacobins' fall from power

There were five directors
                        who ran things

helped by a bicameral
legislature.

     Britain, Russia, Austria, Naples, Portugal
     and Turkey

     united to war against the
                   French Republic

The Directory
     was known for its
          fiscal corruption

& lost the faith-will required to survive

                           ✴

     In 1796
     the French armies
     had become the
          armies of Napoleon

The Rev, for now, was defeated
by moneyed people inside France
and by the coalition of Euro-tyrannies,
the Absolutists, the Royalists,
     fans of the Clergy and
the complexes of leeching nobility.

                           ✴

Bonaparte

Napoleon overthrew The Directory in 1799
and for 15 years thereafter
     was the autocrat of France
          and the lands he conquered

He crowned himself Emperor
                    in front of the Pope
                              in Paris

*

Retreat from Moscow

After a 12-week campaign in 1812
                    with 100,000 troops
Napoleon entered Moscow
          to find it in flames
                    3/4 ths of the city
                              destroyed within a week

He stayed in Moscow till Oct 18
waiting for tsar Alexander I
                    to cringe for peace

*

Invaders from the West
                    stumble in the snow.
An early winter
          snared his men
          killing the horses
 and thousands of soldiers
                    in foodless winterless garb

The Russians
          chased the French
 and nearly captured Napoleon in Lithuania
                    on the horsekilling ice
                              of the Beresina River

5

The Romanovs

The Romanovs
ruled Russia
from 1613 to 1917—
Some were sane &
some were bonkers

Alexander I, the tsar from '01–'25
was the son of the Mad Tsar Paul I,
who was murdered
with Alexander's "connivance"
according to the
           Penguin Dictionary of Modern History

Alex was a hero
in the battle against France:
On 3-31-'14
     he invaded Paris.

As for the way he governed
at first he made some liberal reforms,
but believed God had chosen him to lead the world
and sank in the drool of reaction

    Alexander was subject
    to periods of religious mania
    It was reported Alex
           did not actually die in '25
        but fled to be a hermit
    His coffin was opened in '63
           and found a dusty cenotaph

6

Pushkin
(1799–1837)

It takes a hundred years
to hurl aside
          a clinging, ancient order

Pushkin was part of a two-century
                    Chant for Change

in whose second centennium
                    still we chant.

          Pushkin was an "iskra,"
          a spark, who lived in the open age
          of Byron, Shelley Goethe, Égalité, Fraternité
          when bards seized freedoms underused.

          He wrote on a variety of themes
                    impossible to publish
                              later on in the century

Pushkin's poem "Poslanie k tsenzoru"   (Epistle to the Censor)
His 1819 "The Village" attacked serfdom
"Noel" 1818 ridiculed Alexander I

The minister of war Arakcheyev
is "scorned" in the epigram
                    "Against Arakcheyev"

          His very daring "Ode to Liberty"
                    was passed from hand to hand
                    in manuscript

          The soldiers in the barracks
                    could chant it from memory

They almost fried Pushkin in Siberia
                    for "Ode to Liberty,"

but he took a gig in Kishinev
                    in Bessarabia
          (site of the Pogrom 83 years later)

for two years, to avoid it.

                    *

          Touching France
          France touches you

                    *

During the wars 'gainst Napoleon
          the soldiers and officers
                    were exposed to the
                              revolutionary ideas of the West

Some officers adopted the
concept then in vogue in France, Germany and Italy
that the safest way
          for guaranteeing political progress
                    was through secret societies.

Sec-soc's began to be formed in Russia
                              around 1816,
          a year after Waterloo.

          Puskin had friends associated with
          the pre-Decembrist
                    secret political societies
          such as the Union of Salvation

          He became a member of the Green Lamp
          which in addition
                    to wild partying
          may have been part of

a pre-Decembrist sec-soc:
                 The Union of Welfare

It's hard to trace
            the members of a successful sec-soc

        and the revs
                    never quite
        trust a poet

but when tsar Alexander I died suddenly
in Taganrog on 12-1-'25
                    (or fled to be a hermit)
                            without an heir,
some officers from the secret societies started a mutiny,
under the leadership of one Paul Pestel.

Thirty officers supported by three thousand soldiers
tried to prevent the senators from taking an oath of allegiance to
new tsar Nicholas I.

The Decembrists had hoped
the rest of their garrison might
                    rush to their side

Instead their fellow soldiers
                    turned and fired,
                            and dozens were dead.

All the leading conspirators they could locate,
including Pestel, were hanged.

        When the take-over failed
        Pushkin rushed to his pad
                    and burned some compromising papers

            and began to position himself
                        with the new tsar.

In 1826 Nicholas
summoned Pushkin to Moscow and
        announced that he, the tsar, henceforth'd
                be Pushkin's personal censor,

while at the same time
the tsar placed him under the close surveillance
of secret police chief Benckendorff

        Nicholas I
        forced Pushkin
        to wear the uniform of the
                Gentlemen of the Chamber
        in the final years to his life,
                to Pushkin's great resentment.

No contemptible tsar-barf
could stop the liberal thought-waves of the 18th century
        Liberté, Égalité, Fraternité
                        from lifting the boats.

Pushkin Pushkin!
        Liberté Égalité Poetry Fun
Pushkin Pushkin!

The Revolution
        is as absolute
                as tsar this-and-that

& Pushkin was stretching
                the drumskin on the frame

7

The Russian Police State

Meanwhile, Nicholas I ruled for
                        thirty hideous years

(1825–1855)
He set up a police state apparatus,
        the infamous "Third Section," in 1826
                        to prevent revolutionary ideas
                                        oozing from abroad

Revolution
        "in all its forms"
                (such as freedom of expression)
                                was to be stomped
his severe and misanthropic face
                        ever wincing
                                at the concept of change.

He put into place very strict press censorship,
and a system of passports making it difficult
                        for Russians to visit other countries.

He discouraged the growth of
                        universities and schools

His secret police were always in action,
stirring and spying and spoiling.

Composers, of course, were suspect
                and musical works were examined
                        out of fear the notes
                                might be done
                                in a rev-code.

He made his courtiers cut their beards
        because beards were a sign of
                democratic sympathies in Western Europe

                        *

Rurality, which should have meant an easy life,
                                meant poor-kill.
Now and then there were peasant rebellions
                which opened the window
                        and forced a temporary discussion

31

of the peasants' grim life.

Then clank, then clunk,
Then thut-thut,
    window shut

*

Nationalism to Avoid Justice

Russia controlled 1/6th of Gaia
and one way the people
            will shudder into a kind of
                        unanimity
is through beating at borders
            rousing the hate for Others
                        and Russifying the vast
1/6th of Gaia the tsar controlled.

So there was a deliberate, relentless Russification
of the hugeness—the whole of Siberia,
            and in central Asia to Tashkent, Samarkand,
                        Bokhara, Khiva and Kokand;

and in the Caucasus, from the Black Sea to the Caspian.

Russia was a moiling mix ,
            with 87 million Orthodox Greek
            5.2. million Jews
            13.9 million Muslims
            430,000 Buddhists
                        and hundreds of
                        schisms and sects

            the Russian Orthodox church
            was determined to smash
                        with its iron ikon
                  till all bent down
            in fealty to the iron triad

of Tsar, Church, Absolute Authority.

Repression
    is the craftshop
        of the drumskin

8

Euro-Rev 1848

In 1848
Michael Bakunin wrote to his sister
            from exile in Paris,
  "We shall not be happy
    till the whole world is in flames"

French was the *lingua revolutionis*
and everybody looked to Paris
       for the flamma aeterna
    of working people betterment

France was now a republic
and it had done away with things like debtors prison.

      1848 huge unemployment—
          a slump—
          one of the
          periodic blessings
              of a greed economy.

French workers wanted
    the gov't to help organize
        useful guaranteed work
    at wages and benefits
        families could live on

*

National Workshops

The French gov't decreed
                on Feb. 26, '48
National Workshops
be set up to give employment to
                out-of-work workers

100,000 came to Paris
        from the provinces
             for the Workshops

The right hated the workshops
as much as the U.S. right
          hated the WPA and the CCC

and wormed within
          to stomp it down.

*

The First Workers' Congress in the World

What was known as the Luxembourg Commission
met in Paris
and the very first day
      they ordered the workday to be lowered
      to 10 hours in Paris
      and 11 in the provinces.

The Luxembourg Commission
proposed setting up all over France
      agricultural colonies
      each with a hundred families
      with a common laundry
      and big kitchen
         where wholesome food
           would be prepared
            for the colony

Other colonies were to be created
by industrial workers
        who would borrow sufficient money
        from the state
                to become self-sufficient

These colonies were to have a full system
of social security for illness
                and old age.

Only one such cooperative was ever formed.

                *

Russia already
had in place for centuries
a system of cooperatives
                called the Artel.

So that when workers
came to a city
        from a province
say, to work as carpenters or masons
they united in groups of ten to fifty people
lived in a house together
ate together & each paid his part of the costs
to the elected elder of the Artel.

All over Russia
        "since time immemorial"
                a system of Artels.

                *

Waiting for Signs from France

The King of France, one Louis-Philippe
was 75 and thought soon to die
his health was waning

and people all over awaited his passing

certain the twists of his agonized sheets
were the twists
            to trigger the rev

In South America Garibaldi
        was waiting this sign
            to bring him back
                    for the liberation of Italy

but the people of Paris of '48
tossed out the living king
who ran with the queen
through a back door
            in the Tuileries
            and headed for England.

The drums were heard
                    without borders
& the students of Germany
the patriots of Italy and Hungary
            arose to the
            drum-thrums of rev

Poland, northern Italy and Ireland
        hungered to be free of foreign domination

There must have been fifty revolutions
        erupting in Europe in '48

in the small German and Italian states
        in the provinces of Austrian empire

in Poland, in Bohemia, in Paris

            the hunger for rev
            the hunger for rev

                    *

The Issue of a German Parliament

In 1848
a group met in Heidelberg to
              organize a parliament
to represent the entire, splintered
              German nation

The German people had never had elections
and the group called for them

*

The Communist Manifesto

written in German
was published in
    early 1848

and soon began its long
censorious enceinturement

*

Austria

The Austrian monarchy—the Hapsburgs—
ruled Austria, Hungary, Bohemia, Northern Italy,
and a big chunk of Poland.

The Hapsburgs dread-hated the workers &
intellectuals.

The exploiting classes
kept Austrian workers
              stomped in the abyss

There were large factories
                and tremendous poverty

dead tired workers in dead toned rooms

*

The Etiquette of Absolutism

In Austria
          the E. of A.
forbade the Emperor
                from giving any reasons
                          for his decisions

*

Censorship in Austria

Every single book, paper
or advertisement
in the Austrian Empire
had to be approved
by the censor

In Vienna
12 guys could handle
the censorship,
          showing how few the
          publications were

*

The Rev o' '48

All in all
      it was a tossing of

        violence 'gainst violence

The heat of the Dream
        was not enough
to shatter the old order
        so that new more-benevolent pieces
could form in
        a better pattern.

After a failed rev
        there's that dreaded thing
called "reaction"

when the greed-heads,
        repressionist clergy,
    bruised egos,
        right wing nuts
and score-settlers

        pour dirt

9

Hard Times for Dostoevsky

In 1847 the writer Belinsky
        sick with consumption
            and staying with Turgenev
                in Salzbrunn
                    for the cure
wrote a famous letter to Gogol
    —a "furious invective"
        against serfdom, the
            creepiness of the
Russian Orthodox church,
and the ghastly geekiness
        of the state bureaucracy.

This letter was passed about in
          thousands of handwritten copies

and became the
          Manifesto of Russian Liberalism.

Anyone reading this
letter aloud to others
          in Russia
could suffer the death penalty
yet most of the intelligentsia
knew it
          almost by heart

The Secret Police
hated the
          concept of
                    "The Circle"

In November of '48 there began
          what was known in police reports as
                    the Petrashevsky Circle

A group of young intellectuals
met Friday evenings
     in the library
          at Mikhail Petrashevsky's house
in Petersburg.

The library had the works of Fourier,
Proudhon, Marx, Feuerbach
                    and others.

The base of the meetings
was the hunger for
          representative democracy
and various propositions for
                    communal economics.

The tsar shook his epaulets in anger
          when the secret police told him about it.

At one of the meetings of the
Petra' ◯

Dostoevsky was chosen
to read Belinsky's Letter to Gogol.

That was the main ground for his arrest.

On April 23, '49 Dosto and his brother
and 30 others were popped

On December 22
they were condemned to death
and were driven to
a large outdoor
execution zone

and just when the soldiers
were about to fire
the tsar commuted the sentence to Siberia

Dost. was sent to Omsk for 4 years
hard time 'mong hard timers.

and another six years of exile
before he could return
to the literary life
of Moscow or St. Petersburg

There's nothing quite like
a few years in Siberia
to calm the passion for rev

and focus the
inner scream.

✳

Two years later
on Dec. 2, '51

41

Napoleon's nephew
then President of France
seized total power

made himself emperor
& intellectuals
        all over France
                invisibly puked

It buffed the soul of
Baudelaire
who vowed
        "to remain
                from now on
        aloof from all
                human politics."

*

Dosty, then Baudy, then Turgy

The great Turgenev
—however cautious—
was arrested
for a month
and jailed on
his estate for a year
for publishing
                in '52
an obituary
for the banned Nicholai Gogol.

10

Defeat in the Crimea

There was always the dream
of grabbing land and saving people

especially Christians
        from the Turkish "infidels"

The Ottoman Empire
controlled from the Persian Gulf to Morocco
and from
      Constantinople to the
            approaches to Vienna

It was perceived
      by the 19th Century as weak

Tsar Nick sneered at Turkey as
        "The Sick Man of Europe."
and called for its partition

The other countries
        in the European pond culture
didn't want Russia eating Turkey
and so propped up the Ottoman

The century had already seen
great zeal to free
        the glory of ancient Greece
from Mohammedan culture

The great poet Byron died
       at the siege of Missolonghi
           in April of '24.
and finally Greece
      was made an "independent" state.

           *

1853

Russia made a demand to protect
      Christians within the Ottoman empire,

43

kept shoving at the Turks,
and then there was war.

The French, English and Sardinians
joined with the Turks
                against the Russians

500,000 people died

There was a year-long seige
                of Sevastopol by the allies

The Russians forced
                their conscripts to march
                                in a thanato-trudge
into the Crimea from the north—

        We're Marching to Sevastopol

                The deserts of southern Russia
                were flecked at frequent foot
                with fallen corpses

        We're Marching to Sevastopol

        for Tsar, for God, for glory, for the Holy Synod
        for fear of flogging, for indeterminate senses
                        of why not? &
                                what does it matter anyway?

44

We're Marching to Sevastopol

500,000 people died
          on both sides
till the taking of Sevastopol
in '55
     & Th' Treaty of Paris
            in '56
                in which Russia
                      had to agree
                          to limit armaments
in the Black Sea,
     to withdraw from th' mouth
     of the Danube

and to give back Bessarabia
which it had annexed in 1812.

                    ✳

                Russia faced Euro-snicker
                for its backward ways
                and fumbly style
                in the loss of th' Crimean War
                The Ruling Class was convinced
                that if Russia were to regain
                her prestige as a great power
                and not be snickered at
                      in the semi-changed realms
                                of the West
                some significant changes would
                          have to be made
                in the way Russia was ruled

11

The Chekhov Family

Chekhov's
paternal grandfather
a serf named Yegor Mikhailovich Chekh
(who ran a sugar-beet mill, and
then was the superintendent
of an estate in Voronezh Province in
central European Russia)

bought freedom in 1841
for his wife and three sons
at 700 rubles a head

He hadn't the bread to free-buy his daughter
but good Count Chertkov
tossed in her freedom for measure.

*

A Russian "Cursus honorum":
(1860–1890)

serfdom

↓

shopkeeping

↓

"professions"

*

Yegor apprenticed
            one son to a bookbindery near Moscow

Other sons, Mitrofan and Pavel
opened up small stores in
            a place called Taganrog

In 1854 Pavel Chekh
married Yevgenia Yakolevna Morozova
from a serf background also
            the daughter of a traveling cloth merchant

The family changed from Chekh
            to Chekhov

12

The Emancipation of the Serfs

Just before
America's war
            to free its own,
52 million serfs were "freed"
                        in Russia

The Emancipation Decree, as it was called,
            was dated 19 February 1861
                        when Chekhov was one year old

Overnight they were free to own property,
choose jobs freely, marry whomever they chose

Most landowners did not want to give serfs land
and it was scammed through that
            even though the land had been farmed by
the peasants for centuries,
            and viewed by them as theirs

the land was in fact the property of the "landowners,"
who therefore had to be paid.

*

Greed-heads overestimated the value of the land.
The peasants had no voice in the negotiations
so that each peasant family received less land
than they had previously farmed,
and what they now "owned"
                  was less than needed for
                            even poverty-level subsistence.

*

Read Chekhov's story, "The Peasants"
for what it was like
             never to have enough food
                        in a rich land

*

The state paid the landowners cash,
            and the peasants were supposed to pay the state
for the land for 49 years at 6.5 per cent interest.

*

The Traditional Peasant Commune

The land was handed over to the traditional peasant commune,
with control over it contained in the village assembly, or *Mir* .

Bakunin declared that the Russian peasants were "born socialists,"
and others agreed—

      The *Mir*, the communal body
                    in charge of village affairs

and other traditional collectivist mores
made the Populists hope that Russian socialism
might grow from the villages

and by-pass the road predicted by Marx
that socialism would only come
        after ghastly exploitative capitalism
                and mercantilism
        leading to ghastly proletarian impoverishment
        leading to rev

*

Faith in Nobodaddy

The peasants swayed bitter, bent,
                broke, and bashed

But even the bitter-bent need
        a fascicle of future to
           keep them from
        hacking their masters with scythes
in the rouse of the Now.

The myth of the tsar
        as the Deliverer
was like a drug
        to the Peas'

There was a "blind trust" in the tsar
who was thought to be tricked by the nobles:

"When the tsar finds out what they've done,
                he'll give us land"
        was the grief-groan

as the peasants waited patiently for
    "Tsar Liberator,"
        to set aside his own passivity
                and stir theirs.

*

The Great Reforms

As for the political apparatus,
for ten years beginning in the early 1860s
there were what they called The Great Reforms

Trials by jury
            replaced
                    secret, often hideous, written trials.

There was a slight, but insufficient,
                    relaxation of press censorship

And laws were promulgated
            granting rights to special classes of Jews
to have unrestricted residence
and the opportunity for gov't service

*

Zemstvos

Semiautonomous elected
            local administrative units
                    called "Zemstvos" were set up
                            in rural areas

Under the Zemstvos tsarist Russia offered
free medical, dental and surgical care
                            in village hospitals.

When he became a physician, Anton Chekhov
worked in the Zemstvo hospitals,

and a number of his stories and letters
show how the Zemstvo system worked.

50

*

Russian Class System

Your economic class was
stamped on your passport

*

Thut-Thut

For ten years the
        liberalization loosened the pain
                        and then the door was shut

on the fingers of th' reform.

*

Interlocking Movements

Every kind of reformist,
hesitantist and gradualist
existed in the tangle of
        Interwoven and Interlocking Movements

There were liberals
There were those who looked to France or Germany
There were Nihilists
There were socialists
There was the "conscience-stricken gentry"
There were the "machinations of reactionary landowners"
There were the freed serfs
            looking to wheel-deal
                        or get into the professions
There was a rise in the urban workers
                        predicted by Marx

There was the intelligentsia
There were the ever-stirring secret police
Left wing populists
Right wing populists
                    and any serious work
                    (such as printing a leaflet)
                    was carried out
                    in tsar-dreading secrecy

                    or coded words in literary reviews
                        secret meetings
                            whispered asides

                    & the secret whisper of
                        ink

                            *

        There were reformer and radical
        émigré groups in the cities of Europe

                    who published newspapers & pamphlets
                    where all the banned thoughts
                                could be expressed

        well, most of the thoughts

                            *

Commation in Honor of the Printing Press

        The printing press
                in a police state
        you worship
                as a deity
                    in its secret shrine

        and the
                very, very slight

& secret shuffling sound
as your secret supporter
hands you a wad of ruble notes
by the Kazan Cathedral
        in St. Petersburg
                to print a leaflet

*

Song to the Underground

In a police state
       rules are sneered at
              & dreams of change are nourished

in secret groups

and so it was in Russia
for several centuries

and especially when the
Grand Reform
       policed to a halt.

In the Underground
everything is anything,
that is,
      open to question.

To the rightwing outsider
the *Underground*
is a dome of doom

but to those
       INSIDE the *Underground*
the air, the tone, the clime
      can thrill a person more
            than all the kisses of infinity

In the Underground,
        where freedom is sacred
                and all things
                        open for discussion
let's laugh at the tsar, the pope,
                and even ourselves!

        Fie! Fie! Fie-Fie Fee!
        Nihil Nada Nobodaddy!

In the Underground
        we talk about the family, marriage,
                taxation, the status of women
                        freedom for peasants,
                                Elected Assemblies,
and the varieties of Western socialism:
        Saint-Simon, Bakunin, Proudhon,

        plus the Vast-Village Russian socialism
        that grows, some of us think,
                out of the ways of
                        our vast rurality

and there is nothing
        the secret police can do about it

        Fie! Fie! Fie-Fie Fee!
        Nihil Nada Nobodaddy!

In the Underground
        we have our own form of Ghost Dance
                We're with them—
                        the millions of souls once miserable
        from under the dark Russian sod

and there is nothing
        the tsar can do!

        Fie! Fie! Fie-Fie Fee!
        Nihil Nada Nobodaddy

54

13

Go to the People

There was temptation
     to "believe" in the
          bent-down peasants

golden like
     endless wheat
in a 7-century hail.

          *

This was the time
     influential writers
          such as Bakunin and Herzen
pointed to the Russian peasants
          as "born socialists"

It was a tactic
     which read the future like this:
the middles classes
     increasingly admire the West

but our drive is Slavophilic

Our people are not just greedy strivers
We're sincere, we have solidarity,
and the way we already live
          points to socialism!

while the West—
     well, the West is decadent,
poisoned with vice, selfish,
          and suffused with capitalist mania

          *

Of course Anton Chekhov
had some later words
            on the worship of peasants—

"In my veins
    runs the blood of a
            mouzik

& the virtues of a mouzik
do not astound me."

                        ✳

1861

The great Alexander Herzen
published an emigre newspaper in London called
        Kolokol (The Bell)

It was "illegal"
        but smuggled to Russia
                and read by many.

Though Alex II
            had just freed the serfs
he took repressive measures
                        against the universities

Herzen was the first
            to urge young people
                        to "go to the people."
                        (idti v narod)

"Go to the people. This is where you belong
            exiles from science, soldiers of
                        the Russian nation."

It was the drumskin of the next generation.

*

1862

Land and Liberty (Zemlia i Volia) was founded,
influenced by the ideas of
            Chernyshevsky, Belinsky and Bakunin.

determined to bring about rev
through propaganda,
            with assassination being classified as propaganda.

To Zemlia i Volia
            violence would speed up th' transformation—

that you couldn't rely on
            a vast, swaying mass of
                        illiterate peasants.

The working class was, as yet, small
and the bourgeoisie yet too weak
            even to think of selling out.

*

Therefore the revs
    had both to educate
        and to rouse
           the victims

of the tsarist Nobodaddy

*

Hell in '66

There was a short-lived group
in Moscow called "Hell"

a member of which
    tried to kill the tsar in '66

*

The Okhrana

The tsar hastened rightward
and he set up the dreaded Okhrana,
a secret police replacing the former Third Section.

The first head of Okhrana, 1866–1874
    was Count P. A. Schuvaloff

*

    but nothing could stop
    the blood on the drumskin
        now and again
    an action
        an outbreak
           & blood-spattered
    sticks on the skin

＊

And then, à la Beatnik,
arose the phenomenon
named Nihilism

which people regarded
as the most
serious of all
        revolutionary problems

heh heh heh

The right wing press
        always posts its pejoratives:

"Nihilist" "Beatnik," "Hipster,"
"Yippie," "Commie," "SDSer"

                heh heh heh
                danger
                heh heh heh

14

The Revolutionary Catechism

The revolutionary is a doomed human
She has no personal interests
        He has no business affairs or emotions
She has no attachments or property
        He has no name
Everything
        is focussed upon
                a single thought
                        a single thrill
                                a single love:

REVOLUTION

Dum spiro pro revolutione spero

Turgenev first used the name "Nihilist"
                              in *Father and Children*
                                        in 1862
        In Russian it's: нигили́зм

Also in the early '60s the first Russian edition of
The Communist Manifesto
        translated by Bakunin

and then, in '69, *The Revolutionary Catechism*
                              was writ and passed around
                              among the revs

        Oh Nihilism
                let's tear it down and pulverize!
                It's evil and rotted

        Oh Flames of Nihil!
        Sacredly flaming,
                Burn down this filth of Tsar
                              and flogging Count,
                of literary hack and secret police

        Burn it & sack it, O Nihil!

Nihilism
the triumph of the completely rootless individual
Nihilism
deny the order, crush the order, break the order
Nihilism
free from all social and moral bonds
Nihilism
no relationship with any society
                              other than freezone Nihilism
Nihilism
complete independence, as Lone One's Loning

There's only so long
        that greed-heads
                can op
                        without
                serving the potatoes
                        of class warfare

The flamma revolutionis could not be denied
The flamma of class strife
The flamma that so horrified the right wing cartoonists
The flamma

 to tear down the old order
 to tear it down
 to trample down the centuries of serf-beating vom

                Flamma Aeterna
                        In Plato's cave
                        & its clusters of sentience

                        no peace no peace
                        till all
                                are free fed and fed free
                Flamma Aeterna

Break it down tear it down
and the exploiters will reconnoiter

Dum spiro pro revolutione spero

& then break down the new order of exploiters
                                again and again
                        century 'pon century

Dum spiro pro revolutione spero

Till the spires of Sharing arise
                        in the black soil

Dum spiro pro revolutione spero

15

Taganrog

In a zinc-roofed one-story house
    with green shutters
        on Police Street in Taganrog
            Anton Pavlovich Chekhov was born

to Pavel and Yevgenia Chekhov
on January 17, 1860.

Taganrog, a "city" of around 60,000
        in South Russia,
            600 miles from Moscow
        on the northeast shore of the Sea of Azov,
                itself an inlet of the Black Sea.

Once a big port for the export of grain
        by Chekhov's childhood
            the harbor was silted up

It had the proverbial "gentle inertia"
        of provincial Russia

a polluted water type of town
        where life was "eked out"
    and some of its store signs were misspelled

and where Life itself
        was spelled
           Li(listless)fe and
           Li(brutal)fe

Prisoners from the town jail
        pulled carts with produce
            from street to street

or searched out stray dogs

in the marketplace
and clubbed them with spikèd sticks

in the gazing eyes
of the young man
whose life was spent evolving
from spikes and sticks

*

Not much style
but masses of mud
and a moil of nationalities
in a grain port.

Most of the wealthy grain merchants were Greeks,
and while brutality and boredom etched the city,
Taganrog at the same time was the cultural center
for the surrounding Cossack and Ukrainian boondocks—
There was a cathedral, a new public library,
a bandshell at the town park, a theater,

& even with its public flogging
and broken swords
he always felt the "odi et amo" of Catullus
for his home town,
Taganrog,
Sea of Azov

*

Chekhov was relish
in a sibling sandwich,
some younger some older.

Alexander born in 1855, Nikolai in 1858,
Ivan in 1861, Maria in 1863
and Mikhail in 1865.

*

Memory

His earliest memory
        was hitting hands

"Every morning as I awoke
        my first thought was,
                'Will I be beaten today?' "

After a hitting by daddy,
        Chekhov was made to kiss
                the hitter's hand

*

Father Ran a Store

Father ran a store
a dark and dirty store
with coffee, candles, sunflower seeds & oil,
groceries, tobacco, nails, tea, flour,
sweets and lamps and wicks
        and vodka

There was a black sign
        with gold letters over the door:

TEA, SUGAR, COFFEE AND OTHER GROCERIES—
TO TAKE HOME OR DRINK ON THE PREMISES.

The store was open from 5 AM till 11 PM
At night it was a scrounge-lounge
        for the tale-telling yokels.—

Anton sometimes tended the store at night.
    He'd refill the vodka crock
        and Mozart the million-fibered tales of a port town
            grim, grainy, groany, groiny and graspy

        from liquor-loosened lips.

Daddy liked to pray a lot
and scam the peasants

One of his favorite store-bore apothegms
was, "Wares without owners go weeping."

One day a rat drowned in a barrel
of cooking oil
and daddy brought in a priest
who chanted a purification
ritual above the oil of rattus rattus

so father could sell it.

It was the type of childhood
you count the days to escape

"For us, childhood was sheer suffering."

*

The Floor as a Drum

Dad would take them a couple hours early
to church

and then the family would file home
for the mid-morn break

and sing the hymns just heard
in front of the ikons

Daddy would have them
lie on the floor
praying and beating their
heads on the planks
in a thumping susurrus

till it was time once again
     to trudge to the final morning mass.

                    *

     Mom was a good story teller
     and father was skilled
                    in making adornèd ikons
     He read French novels
     and taught himself the violin

     For a while he had a tutor in
     French
                    come to the house for the kids

                    *

     1867
          Volume One
               Das Kapital

     Not many copies in Taganrog

                    *

     It was such a police state
     that Anton's Latin teacher
     at the Taganrog Russian Gymnasium
     spied among the teachers
                    for political plots
     and sent off denouncements to the police

                    *

                '69 & '70

     When he
          was 9
     The Revolutionary Catechism

66

                          was written
            and when he was 10
            Vladimir Ilyich
            Ulyanov
                    (Lenin)
                    was born.

                          *

                Visuality

        In towns from Sumer and Akkad
                        to Taganrog and Tuscaloosa
        every birth, death, and event is everybody's business.

        So in Taganrog
        the ultrasmart townie named Anton
        knew it all—
        each muddy alley, every building and spire
        each smell, each moil, each mell—

        The secret mind began to whisper,
                    to sort, to sift, to store
                        the billion-fold feast of particulars

                          *

            In Mitrofaniyevksy Square
                    ta-tum
            ghastly public killings
                    ta-tum ta-tum
            where they broke a sword
                    ta-tum
        on the condemned one's head
        to the rattle of sticks on doom-skins

        a view little Anton could see and hear
            from his nearby window.

                                                        67

sledding
in the
town park
smearing his ears
    with goose fat
to keep them from
      freezing

16

The Thrill of Grease Paint

When he was a wild 13, in '73,
he was taken for the first time to the theater
to Offenbach's *La Belle Hélène*.

He *loved* the haunts of hocus pocus and logos,
      the lure of The Other,
went many times to the theater in Taganrog.

He wrote his first playlets
which he and his brothers
    staged at home
      with props and scenery.

    Other.

17

The Triumph of Failure

In 1875
his two older brothers, Alexander and Nikolai,

fled to Moscow.   One became a journalist,
the other a painter.

The next year father Pavel's store
mothed into the debt-flame, and dad fled to Moscow
to avoid debtor's prison.

The mother, Yevgenia Yakovlevna also went to Moscow
with Chekhov's younger brothers, Ivan and Michael
and sister Maria.

Anton stayed behind
from 16 to 19
an emancipated youth
supporting himself by tutoring

and studying
        to pass the tough exams
                    that would give him
free education
        at the university in Moscow.

He gave lessons in the winter
        trudging from house to house
                with leaky boots and a chilly coat

Maybe it was here that the bacillus
                    was coughed into his
chilly lungs
        and sealed
                    in skullèd dormancy

18

Narodniki

While Anton Chekhov
        was living his childhood

                    in Taganrog

        the Narodniki
                    arose from the Russian Underground

        Young people
                    heeding the Underground Press

        to go among the masses

                         *

They learned the Primal Secret
                    of rev-work:
that secret presses
flambent fliers
and inky exhortations
                    did not enter the lives
                              of the bent-down masses

so they decided to
        "go among the people"
                    (idti v narod)

which is how they
                    got the name, "Narodniki"

                         *

                    So that
                    the SDS in
                         1968
                    did not invent
                    the concept of
                       "going to the people"

                    to learn from them
                    & prepare them for
                              a sharing eco-nomos

70

＊

The Narodnichestvo

This peaceful populist movement
the *narodnichestvo,*
        inspired by Herzen and Bakunin—
                        captured the moment

with its devotion to the People:
to bring it all together:
peasant and student
        smooth hand and callused

to heal the chasms
                with peaceful work
construction, teaching, caring

to create a Native Socialism

＊

Famine Roam

In weeks of plenty
the peasants might have
a meal of millet porridge
mixed with hemp-seed oil
                        after field work

but there was a horrible famine
                the season of '73
and oil of hemp gave way
to goutweed soup
stale bread
        moistened in water
& the cold fingers of children
in snowmelt

plucking
      sorrel & clover
         to their
lips.

And when starvation or slumps occurred
the population
        grew mobile & roaming

Workers would leave the country
          and slave in factories
then sleep in starvation's tenements

where it was impossible
      to rest and recover
        after a workday
rarely less than 12, 14, 15, up to 18 hours.

*

1874

The tsarist gov't
had ordered all students studying abroad
to return to Russia by Jan. '74
    (where they wouldn't be
        exposed to
Western ideas, or the
        radical émigré press)

Most came back
   and many joined
      the Narodniki

      —idti v narod.

*

That spring
          2 or 3 thousand students and activists
                    many of them women

     "went to the people"
       serving as teachers, agricultural experts,
       veterinarian surgeons, doctors, nurses
       mechanics, midwives, school teachers, governesses,
       factory hands and laborers.

     They explained their positions
     and handed out their pamphlets
     looking
                    with enormous youthful energy
                                        for converts

                    *

The "Mad Summer" of '74

The campaign of
               idti v narod
                         grew 'mid the growing

The press called it
               the "Mad Summer"

     this intense
               living leaflet
                         of devotion and idealism

                    *

Get Off My Property

The peasants declined the help
 of these voluntary teachers and helpers,

It's difficult enough
            for *actual rev's*
to understand the
            phraseology and abstract principles
of socialism
            much less letterless peasants
                        and worn out factory workers

*

Turgenev's *Virgin Soil*
        about the Narodniki
                among the peasants

The Narod's didn't dig it
                and scorned Turgenev

*

Don't Stop, Don't Stop

In '75 thousands returned
            to the villages
and several thousand young people
            were jailed.
Many of the accused imprisoned or exiled without a formal trial.
Some were not put on trial till '78
Scores died in dungeons, some went insane

*

Medicine

In June of '75
        when he was 15,
Chekhov
        swam in a cold river
                on an outing in the country

and came down with peritonitis.
He was cared for by a Dr. Strempf with
    such compassion and skill
                he decided to become a doctor.

*

        By 1876
various splintery Populist groups began to forge
a theoretical and practical common agenda:

- Large estates were to be split up
  and divided among the peasants

- More power for the village assemblies
  and greater local autonomy

The organization, because of police terror, had to be secret,
divided into regions, with secret presses, and large numbers of
sympathizers.

*

1876

There was a second version
of Land and Liberty (Zemlia i Volia)
(The original had occurred in '62)

with a clear program:

- kill tsarism "from below"
- promote strikes among workers
- passive resistance among peasants
- "fighting units" to
            form the vanguard
                    of the rev

*

Action Faction, Praxis Axis

In 1879 Land and Liberty split into two groups.
One was *Chernyi Perediel*
(Black [Earth] Distribution or Black Partition)
with a plan of agrarian socialism, lead by George Plekhanov.

Black Earth stressed the triune importance
of education, propaganda and agitation
among the masses.

The second, larger group was
Narodnaia Volia
(The People's Will),
which believed a mass uprising was impossible,
and that the only way to a democratic government
in the Russian autocracy
would come through killing gov't leaders.

The People's Will's Executive Committee
voted to kill the tsar for failing to set up a
Representative Government.

19

Med School for Anton

In April of '77
Anton visited Moscow for Easter
and was horrified to find his family
sleeping on a single mattress
in a rented room

His father nevertheless
had a list of rules
on the wall

and beat the younger kids
for transgressions

But Dad was drinking
          instead of looking for work.
There was no money to
                    send Maria to school
One of his older brothers had seduced
a married woman, who'd left her husband for him.

     The med student
               knew it was his destiny
                    to lead his family intact
                              out of poverty

                    *

1879

Anton graduated from high school
     (One of his final exams
                    required him to spiel for three hours
          on the topic: "There is nothing
                              worse than Anarchy")
He moved to Moscow
               to study medicine at the university

In med school he received a stipend
               of 25 rubles a month
                    from the city of Taganrog.

Young, brilliant, self-contained
he scanned the stutter of his family
               and took over leadership

They'd been living in the basement
               of a tenement
                    in the red light district

with the tiny windows
          showing at night
               the loitering feet of hookers

They took in boarders
        so that ten people lived in a single room!

His two older brothers, Alexander and Nicolai,
led "independent lives." His dad by then worked elsewhere
and visited once a week.

At home were his two younger brothers, Ivan & Mikhail,
younger sister Maria, and mother Eugenia,
                                        plus boarders.

Anton took over,
        forced them to move to a better pad,
saw that Maria and Mikhail went to school
                        instead of house-moping

and banned corporal punishment
                and the lists of rules
                        from the visiting father.

                        *

        Chekhov apparently had
        a Creeley-like
        hunger for order
                of personal array.

                        *

First Ink

December 24, 1879, Chekhov's first ink!!
        A short piece, "Letter to a Learned Neighbor,"
                                in a mag named *Dragonfly*

20

Ha-Ha Mags

His older brothers both
        submitted to the Ha-Ha mags
so, purely for scratch,
from 1880 to 1885
he wrote around 300 humorous works
        'neath numbersome names:

      A. Ch-te
    Anche
      A. Tchekhonte
      Antosha Tchekhonte
  Antonson
        Baldastov
 My Brother's Brother
        A Doctor Without Patients
 A Quick-Tempered Man
    A Man Without a Spleen
    Rover
      Ulysses

21

The People's Will

In '78 there was the
      "Trial of the 193" Narodkniki
        in St. Petersburg
        with sentences given out
so cruel
      a heave of disgust
        rippled throughout the culture

*

The Executive Committee
of People's Will
(Narodnaia Volia)
announced in its sec-pub
it would kill the tsarist functionaries
conducting the suppression.

*

Then the People's Will
under the leadership of Sophia Perovskaia
and A.I. Zheliabov
began their executive action

Feb. '79, killed Prince Kropotkin, Gov-Gen of Kharkov
Mar. '79 unsuccessful attempt on General Drenton,
head of The Third Section
April '79 attempted killing of Governor of Kiev
May '79 Arkhangelsk Chief of Police stabbed
Sept. '79 they sentenced the tsar to death
Nov. '79 they tried to derail the royal train
Feb. '80 the banquet hall of the Winter Palace
was blown up just as the tsar and family
were about to sit down to a party
60 guards were killed

*

When in '79 a member of Zemlia i Volia
named Soloviev
tried to kill Alexander II

Jews were forbidden
to live in Moscow

Chekhov was in med school
and one of his friends
the painter Isaac Levitan
had to move with his family

to a village outside Moscow
and come by train each day
                    to the School of Painting.

*

Assassination

On Sunday March l, 1881
tsar Alexander II's
        horse drawn sledge
                    passed by a cheese factory
on a side street

The first bomb thrown killed
                    the tsar's two guards
Alexander went to help the men

The second bomb killed him.

        The history books never
        mention the fate of the
                            horses

22

Pogroms and Reaction

        The right wing did very poorly
        protecting the tsar
        but managed
        to crush the People's Will
                    in the next two years

Five members of
Narodnaia Volia were executed.

Others were sent to Siberia.
Some were imprisoned for decades
in the dungeons of Schlusselburg fortress.

*

Long-living rumors
        stippled with people-pain
were always
            part of life
                    in the rural parts of Russia

So that when Alex II was bombed
the rumor flicked
            through th' sticks
            he'd been killed
by landlords to prevent
                    new land distribution

or that the Jews and landlords
in cahoots

killed the tsar
to reintroduce serfdom

& that a secret imperial decree (ukaz)
had been promulgated
            allowing for attacks on Jews.

(The same rumor was spread
            twenty-two years later,
                during the Kishinev pogrom)

                *

Pogroms

Pogrom is Russian for "devastation."

Within a few weeks of the tsar's death
the government inspired
a series of pogroms—

The right wing press
            stabbed forth
                again and again
that some in People's Will were Jewish

                *

Pogrom agitation was
spread by handbills and posters
tacked on fences, walls, trees
            or tossed in the streets
calling on people
            to go after the Jews

                *

Townies, unemployed workers
& wandering mouziks looking for jobs

ransacked Jewish homes and shops,
doing the My Lai:
        rapes, murders, beatings

The police were slow, slow
           to stop it.

          *

Almost 5 million Jews
        lived in the Pale of Settlement
the legal zone set up
        through the centuries
              where they were made
                   to reside

(In '35 the Pale had been
clearly defined: Lithuania, White Russia
—that is, Vikbsk and Mogilev minus the
villages, Little Russia, New Russia,
and the Baltic provinces)

and with the pogroms of '81
thousands of Jews fled to the boundaries
                of the Pale

crossing into the German frontier
        the Bohemian frontier
             the Rumanian frontier

          *

The Manifesto of April 28, 1881

The new tsar
        the magnificent Alexander III
announced
he would not discuss the destiny
               of Russia
with anyone but God.

84

*

The Okhrana

The Secret Police expanded
                                after
                                        th' tsaricide

Okhrana agents were everywhere
They watched every train station
Agents were disguised as
                                bellhops in every hotel
Agents worked as ushers in theaters
They excelled at the *agent provocateur*
All mail was opened and read
There was a 24-hour store in St. Petersburg
        used to supply agents with disguises any time

*

In May of '82
a bunch of "temporary rules"
(which lasted 30 years
                and led to massive emigration)
prohibited Jews
                from buying or leasing land
or moving from towns to villages
or doing biz on Christian holy days

The gov't wanted to keep them
                away from the peasants.

Then quotas were set up
                limiting Jewish access
to secondary and university education
to legal and medical professions
to municipal and local governments.

All of it stirred by the Okhrana

and a psychologically demonic
multi-century knownothingism
                    that pickled rural & townie brains
          by the tens of millions

                    *

Reaction Time

Eras of right wing "reaction"
seem to foam forth
                    every few decades.

Those to whom the word "No,"
thundered forth with
a thousand exclamation points,
!!,
is the sweet tune of angels,

always rise up,
          as far as they can,
                    with their
          tsk-tsking neantifications.

          Russian society
          was in the iron grasp
          of a multigrade bureaucracy
                              known as the Chin.

          The Chin was a highly disciplined
           group of guys
           who strutted around
                    in splendid uniforms
           with golden-fringed shoulders
           and chests made important
                              with ribbons and medals.

          The Chin had a network of grades
          divided into 14 levels:

Civil Branch	*Military Branch*
Imperial Chancellor	Field Marshall
down to	down to
College Registrar	ensign

Everybody from the eighth rank upward
was automatically
raised to the nobility.

In the ranks of the Chin,
the hereditary nobility
and rightist officer corps,
a belief was formed
that Nihilism, Rev, and, shudder shudder,
Anarchism
came from the secular spirit—

from a sense of being citizens of Europe
or the world

and rev's only remedy
(as in the early part of the 19th century)
lay in the dungeony triad:
Nationality, Orthodoxy and Autocracy.

*

The plan was to
force th' Russian language and culture
on the nationalities and ethnic groups
in the empire

such as Finland, Baltic provinces, Polish- and the Yiddish-
speaking southwest provinces,
Tatar-speaking muslims in the Crimea,
and others

*

Therefore there was a systematic
                police-state persecution
    of Jews, schismatics and so-called heretics.

                            *

                The Wobblies used
                to talk about OBU
                One Big Union—

                This was OBR

                One Big Russia

                and way before Lenin

23

Konstantin Petrovich Pobedonostsev
(1827–'07)

Pobedonostsev was a professor of constitutional law
                            at Moscow U

He tutored the sons of Alexander II
and drilled into the tsarlings'
                late-Romanov minds
                    his right wing viewscapes

In 1880 he was appointed the lay head of
the Russian Orthodox Church
                (Procurator of the Holy Synod)
        a position he filled till the pre-rev rev of '05

He had such a grip on the tsars that
from 1881 through 1904
Konstantin Petrovich Pobedonestsev virtually RAN Russia
He could hire and fire government ministers

He was the J. Edgar Hoover of his era,
only worse.

"Parliaments," he said,
"are the greatest lie of our time."
Dostoievsky may have based
The Grand Inquisitor
in *The Brothers Karamazov*
on Pobedonostsev

Any personal opinion was subversive.
Suspicion was the nation's motto.
No more women in higher educational courses
Secondary schools only open to children of the rich
No more administative autonomy in the universities.
The strictest possible censorship.

*

He persecuted religious groups
such as the Dukhobors
Tolstoy intervened
and helped them emigrate to Canada
and the United States

"The mad clamor for a Constitution
spells the ruin of Russia."
— K.P. Pobedonostsev

*

Chekhov and the Summer of '82

Tall
broad shouldered
a wide-brimmed black hat

good manners
pumping people
for interesting anecdotes

*

1883

Chekhov was writing a monthly
column called "Fragments of Moscow Life"
which brought him close to crimes
and more importantly
to the painted parades of the stage.

An editor complained
some of his stories
were getting too serious

and then there were final exams
working in clinics
visits to hospitals
the slicing of corpses

and the tossing of ink for the ha-ha's

24

Medical Practice
(1884)

In June Anton Chekhov
finished his medical studies
                and opened his practice

That summer he worked
                in the *Zemstsvo* system
at the rural hospital in the village of Chikino
                                not far from Moscow
        then at another country hospital at Zvenigorod

First fees:
        five rubles for curing a toothache
        a ruble for ridding a monk of dysentery
        three rubles for the upset stomach of
                                a vacationing actress

                        *

He saw the underside
                of peas-pov

the evidence of drunkenness, meanness,
tapeworms, diarrhea, suppurating wounds

how vodka was the crack
                of the underclass.

In September, back in Moscow
                he put a copper plaque by the door:
                        "Anton Chekhov, Medical Doctor."

How thrilling are middle class accoutrements
                                after a youth of pov!

rubles for new chairs and furniture
rubles for a piano
               and evenings of music!
rubles for paying the grocer with cash not credit

though half of his patients, he noted
"I treat for free, and the other half
               give me three or five rubles."

Doing the Whitman—
        publishing his own book,
            The Tales of Melpomene
six stories, 96 pages, 60 kopecks
under the name Antosha Chekhonte

Then just a few months
         after graduating from med school
possibly from exhaustion
     a writer with deadlines
          and so many sick patients

    there came a dry cough
    a bitter taste in the mouth
    and blood-spit for three days.
    "It's not tb," he said.
    "It's likely a ruptured blood vessel."

*

The Drums

TB is almost always caused
by inhalation of infectious material

breathing in in dried residues of droplets
aerosolized by a cough

Droplets
that can remain

suspended in the air
             for long times
and can reach terminal
                         air passages.

Early in the infection
there's
a silent bloodstream
                   spread
seeding
the lymphatic system
& other organs
             throughout the body

It can have long periods of latency
             th' bacillus sealed over with tissue

The most prominent
source of infection
          is a person with
TB prior to diagnosis—
the closer the contact
             and the younger the age
the greater the risk

             Just the sort of disease
             the young doctor
             might have gotten
                      among the poverty

             or it may have lain dormant
                   from his days going house to house
                   as a Taganrog tutor

25

Arise O Workers

1885

Gradually, through the concepts of Workers Circles and Workers Clubs, the workers were organized.

In 1885 was the first mass strike in Russia, in a large textile factory outside Moscow, involving 8,000 workers.

One journalist at the time wrote that "workers are beginning to voice the same demands as the proletariat of Western Europe. The ideas of Marx and the International have begun to infect the Russian proletariat."

1886

Around 35,000 workers in St. Petersburg went on strike for a shorter work day—ten hours.

*

Arise O Anton

In '85
he published 129 stories and sketches

26

Censorship in Late 19th Century Russia

All of his plays and every story
had to be sent to a State censor
before production or printing

Taboo: rad sheets   mean streets
        bed sheets   church cheats

that is, wild sex, any kind of criticism
          of the military or the tsar or
          nobility or church or foreign policy,
          the promotion of land distribution
                        or the riling up of the poor—

      It's not easy to get
              from American libraries
                      the mechanics of that censorship

A good number of Chekhov's stories were either
chopped up by the Nobodaddies
                        or rejected.

      Maybe scholars
              could go into the archives
      late in this century
      and reinstall the cuts
                      of late last century?

                        *

His first run-in came
in '85, when he wrote a one-act play,
On the High Road, adapted from his story, "In Autumn."

It was set in a decrepit inn on a stormy night,
and starred various derelicts.

It was banned *in toto* by a drama censor named
Kaiser von Nilckheim, on the grounds it
was filthy and morbid.

Is *On the High Road* in the post-Sov archives?

                        *

Certain right wing newspapers
such as Alexei Suvorin's *Novoya Vremya*
were exempt from pre-censorship
but the editors were responsible
        if anything objectionable
                blacked the paper

*

Chekhov wrote for *Fragments*,
Nikolai Leikin's well known St. Petersburg humor mag

Leikin would pre-censor Chekhov's stories. If a Chekhov tale,
say, spoke of the peasants being drunk at Easter,
then, scritch scratch, the pencil would edit it out.

Even so, the censor would still blue-pencil sections
that seemed to allude to the tsar, the army, the church,
& eros

*

The censorship agency for printed works
was apparently called "The Bureau of Press Affairs."

*

In early '86
Chekhov's
"For the Information
           of Husbands"
was so badly cut
by the censors
its fee
    in *Fragments*
was reduced by 10 rubles!!

*

Around 1887
He sketched a tale

"The Story of My Patient,"
about a rev
who does underground work
and over time concludes
that the ethical implications
of what he does
                mean more to him
                than the implications
                            of Ideology

He had, in '87, no hope of publishing
anything so lucid and open
                about rev violence

In an 1891 letter to one Mikhail Albov, editor of *The Northern Herald*, Chekhov announced he's sending the story, and said he doubted it would pass censorship: "Once you've read it, you can decide what to do. If you feel the censors will pass it, have it set and announce its publication, but if when you've read it you find my doubts well founded, please return it to me without having it set or read by the censors, because if the censors reject it, it will be awkward for me to send it to a censorship-free publication: once a publisher finds out the story has already failed to pass, he'll be afraid to publish it."

In the fall of '91 he worked more on the story
and read the first few lines
to Suvorin who said he could
never dare to publish it in *Novoya Vremya*,

but in the writer's mode of
                Never Give Up
he revised the manuscript in the fall of '92
(self-censorship) and Vakol Lavrov's
left-liberal *Russian Thought* (Русская Мысль)
published it in Feb. of '93
as "An Unknown Man's Story"—passing through
censorship without a single change.

✳

In a letter to Anna Yevreinova,
            publisher of *Northern Herald,*
in March of '89, he told her he
was working on a novel:

"Oh what a novel! If it weren't for the accursèd censorship
  situation, I'd promise it to you in November.
  There's nothing in the novel inciting anyone to revolution,
  but the censors will ruin it anyway. Half the characters say,
  'I don't believe in God,' it has a father whose son
  has been sent to life-long forced labor for armed resistance,
  a police chief who is ashamed of his uniform, a marshal
  of the nobility whom everyone hates, etc. There's a wealth of
  material for the red pencil."

                    *

In another lengthy story, "Three Years," about the decline
of a family in the mercantile atmosphere of Moscow,

the censors cut a number of sections that talked of religion.

                    *

When he was writing *The Wood Demon,* he
wrote to Suvorin
            "My only fear is that the censors
            won't pass it."

                    *

From Chekhov's 1896 Diary

"N. stayed with me from the 15th to 18th August. He has been
forbidden (by the authorities) to publish anything: he speaks
contemptuously now of the younger G, who said to the new Chief of
the Central Press Bureau that he was not going to sacrifice his
weekly *Nedelya* for N.'s sake and that 'we have always anticipated
the wishes of the censorship'... From me he went on to L. N. Tolstoy."

*

The Censors' power slowly ebbed
          during Chekhov's career.

but right up to the end of his life
such as when he finished *The Cherry Orchard*
great Chekhov
                    groveled his work past
                              the Nobodaddies

*

Censors as Critics

A censor's certificate
was needed
to do *The Lower Depths*
at the Moscow Art Theater
                    in '03

They refused it.

Nemirovich-Danchenko
went to St. Petersburg
                    for Gorky

and fought
with the censors
sentence by sentence
and word by word

Finally they granted
                    permission

Why?
Because the authorities
were sure the play would bomb
                    and have no effect.

*

And now we return
    to Chekhov's early fame

27

1885

On holiday
    at a friend's estate

he was using a sewing-machine lid
                        as a scriptoire.

The peasants
        heard there was a doctor there
& hundreds of them
            came for care
        "I've earned a total of one ruble,"
                he wrote a friend

*

    After a brain-rack sess'
    with a friend
    one of the titles
    for his new book
            (published as *Motley Tales*)
    was
    "Buy This Book or You'll Get
                    A Punch in the Mouth"

*

Getting Noticed

Alexei Suvorin
        right wing press magnate
(former liberal)
        read Chekhov's "The Huntsman"

and asked him to write
        for *Novoya Vremya*, or
                New Times,
his big-time daily.

It was big-time money
                for the first time
—on the level of Hemingway
or Fitzgerald
        writing for the glossy monthlies

                ✳

The celebrated writer Dmitry Grigorovich
who forty years earlier
        had "discovered" Dostoevsky

wrote Chekhov
        in March of '86

urging him to give up his pseudonym:

"You have *real* talent,
        one which elevates you above
        the generation of young writers"

and insisted on Chek's new book,
Varicolored Stories, or
        Motley Tales, Jan. '86,
        appear with his real name

but Anton wrote back it
had already been printed,

and how dissatisfied
         he was with *Motley Tales*

"It's a hodge podge
         an indiscriminate conglomeration
of the tripe I wrote as a student,

PLUCKED BARE BY THE CENSORS
and humor sheet editors.

I have 100s of friends
                  in Moscow
a few of whom are writers

& I don't recall a single one of them
reading my things
         or viewing me as an artist

In the five years I have hung around
newspaper offices
         I have grown used to the
overall view that my writing is insignificant.

I am a doctor, and up to my eyeballs in medicine
so I can't recall working on a story for
                           more than a day

'The Huntsman' which everybody likes
I wrote when I was out swimming."

28

The Glory of Youth Fame

The shy young man of 26
         still not using his own name
                  paid a visit to the Capital:

"I was overwhelmed by the reception
                    extended to me
                              by the Petersburg people.
Welcome, acclaim, glorification—
            all of which scared me,
                    because I had been writing sloppily.
                    In an offhand way.

If I had known that I was being read in this way,
I would not have written so much like a hack."

                              *

I Discovered Chekhov

    Voice A

I discovered Chekhov

    Voice B

No, Rat, I discovered him

    Voice C

What are you saying?
I, in my universal skill,
did him find!

    Voice D

No! no!
        I! I! I! am the one
                who sprouted him from the dimness

29

The Song of the Malevolent Clique

They've babbled in Babylon
                    addled in Akkad
                                    and mumbled in Memphis

            sneering & leering & spearing
            the malevolent literary clique

Through all of the time of letters:
                through Greece, Rome, Byzantium,
                                and the 1302 Florence of Dante—
through Paris, through Pushkin, through Poe

            grousing & groaning & grailing
            the malevolent literary clique

He hated the clans of the literati,
                their stupid intrigues
                                their fierce ambitions
                the gravity pulling
        the drool to their lips
                as they bowed and scraped

The bitten-turnip world of the
                        doomed and elderly scribe
                and the rutabaga tart
                                of the youth-pack hack

            staring & stealing & stoning
            the malevolent literary clique

    As Chekhov wrote to his brother,
    "Newspaper guys suffer from a sickness
    named jealousy. Instead of rejoicing
    in your good fortune,
                    they ooze out their venom!"

Clique Hack A:

I do adore the *eau*
of these euphuistic eulogies—
this twilight twitter—
but only fire can make a fritter

Clique Hack B:

A toad dries
          when the stone falls

Clique Hack C:

He doesn't deserve the book stalls!
He's a hack
He's badly attired
This doctor who thinks
               in a dead man's sack
I hate him, even though
               I've just kissed him
                         and toasted him
                                   the joy of Russia!

All Chant:

I love him
I wrap him in a line

I love him
with cords of ink

          He's safer then
          and soon to sink

               ✳

"Were I to shoot myself,"
          Anton Chekhov wrote,
"it would give great pleasure
          to nine-tenths of
               my friends and admirers."

*

That April of '86
      he yearned to get back
            to St. Petersburg
to savor the once-only thrill
      of being the "latest thing"

but he had no money to spare
and he was exhausted
      from a cycle
            of blood-coughs

but he was afraid
      to be examined by another doctor
"It's not so much the lungs as the throat,"
            he told himself

and, bleeding gone,
      he hastened again to St. Petersburg
            for the fame-flame

*

In the fall of '86
      he brought his sister to the Capitol
            so she too could savor the *Gloire*

30

On the Eve

Lenin's older brother, Alexander,
      was a member of Narodnaia Volia,
            (The People's Will)

They'd met in Alexander's St. Petersburg apt.
to plan the killing of Alexander III

on March 1, the sixth anniversary
        of People's Will killing his father

They'd written a manifesto to be given out
                        upon the tsaricide.

The plotters were arrested
                and at the trial
                        Alexander sought to take the blame:
"I am not afraid to die," he told the court,
"because there is no death more honorable
                than death for the common good."

On May 8, 1887, Lenin's brother
                and four comrades were hanged.
Reading the news in the paper, the 16 year old Lenin cried,

        "I'll make them pay for this! I swear it!"

                        *

        Chekhov talked four hours one night
        with the magnate Alexei Suvorin
        and at 1 AM

        Suvorin made an offer!
        New Times would publish a collection of stories,
        plus fork over an advance of 300 rubles
                                against new stories.

        Ahh the thrill!
                beyond just a concept,
                        of a literary ruble-thrust!

        The collection, I believe, was *At Twilight*.

        He leaped back to Moscow,
        tossed off three stories, then
        made a sacred list of 16 others
        he intended to write and mailed the package
        to Suvorin.

Then, energied with cash,
Chekhov spent his advance
on a trip to his boyhood city
of Taganrog

*

The Lure of Traveling and Fleeing

Every now and then
throughout his career
the seething genius fled

He was easily bored
and craved complications—
the more complications
the more material for short stories

and, the grandson of serfs
who'd been slaves
to one piece of land
at least since the early 17th century
had a hatred of shackles.

There was the constant pressure
of his cash-starved family
& the attention-dazing fact-blizzards
of the literary world,

& the need of a doctor's mind
ever dyed with the dying
to flee in the name of *mens sana*.

Raw Thrill is always the finest thrill
and in his early career
no thrill out-thrilled
the one-time excitement
of visiting places
where he was famous

and where the marching bands
        of honor and accolade
            (for at least the first visit)
                would oompah
                        his arrival

                    *

When Lenin
        went to Kazan U
                in the fall of '87

he was drawn
almost at once
            to student disorders

Ahh, student disorders!
when you are
            not yet bewebbed
by career and family
dust and duty

Ahh, student disorders!
when you stand
                at the
                Outer Surface

and dare to gaze
            at Eternity

Lenin was thrown out of school
                    after three months
and escorted by the police
                    to the city limits

                    *

That same fall
Chekhov was troughed in depression—
a three-week "cowardly melancholy"
                    as he called it

and decided to write himself out of
                              the Down Zone
      with the play,
              that took ten days to finish:
              Ivanov

A man named Fyodor Korsh owned
a theater in Moscow
and had been urging
                    Anton to do a play

*

The Aeschylus Option

It's as ancient as
Aeschylus
        designing and directing

or Shakespeare
        sweating
              a perf of *Hamlet*

the insistent, demanding
insertion of
        the writer
into his/her play's production.

Chekhov sweated *Ivanov*
He argued with actors
"I'm constantly at war with them—
had I known,
        I'd never have gotten involved in it."

Sure, Anton, sure
You with
        your hunger for greasepaint
                              and lissome allure.

Then came the play's premiere
to a full house
            at the Korsh Theater
                    November 19, 1887

31

The Rubles of Ivanov

1.

Chekhov
was promised
8%
of th' box office
for the premiere run
of *Ivanov*

& eagerly
tallied the possible cash

It looked
like the then huge
            6,000 rubles!!

Sacred Russia!

2.

Then
the rehearsals,
supposed to be 10,
were cut to 4

uh oh

3.

On opening night
some of
the actors
    ad libbed
  forgotten lines
& were drunk
by Act IV

Thespis forbid

4.

Though there were
            curtain calls
at the end of several acts,

the final act
brought tensions of yes-no,
what Chekhov called
"applausamento-hissing"

so dear later on
        to The Futurists—

There were knuckles on faces,
        hisses and stamping feet,
                spittle and elegant shovings—
till the cops were called
        to cleave 'tween boos and hurrahs

all of which shortened the run,
and a wreck of the rubles for Chekhov

∗

Never Give Up

Ivanov closed after two perf's
& Chekhov went to Petersburg
where he gave a reading
        of *Ivanov*
        to a "literary circle"
        and stared down at his shoes
        during the
                mighty applause
                        at the end

At a dinner party
he met the poet Alexei Pleshcheev
who 38 years before
had been in the
        "Petrashevsky Circle"
                with Dostoevsky

and had stood with Fyodor
before the firing squad
and then just
        before bullet-slam
Nicholas I commuted the off
to soul-twist Siberia.

32

1888

He began his great story, "The Steppe"
in January
        It was published in March
                        in the *Northern Herald*
        to the shouts of "Genius! Genius!"
                        from public and critic

*

The Lure of Natural Beauty for Writing

In May, he rented a dacha on an estate, in the Ukraine,
near the village called Luka
                        on the Psyol River.

There was more room
                for the 8-person family
                                he supported

                    ✳

The Lure of Lissome Grease Paint

After the round-the-clock work
on "The Steppe"

he fluffed forth
a one-act farce, *The Bear*,
                a great source of royalties

& wrote such "curtain-raisers" as
        The Swan Song &
        The Proposal
in 1888

for the money, and for the lissomeness—
for he seemed always willing to hang out
                            with beautiful actresses.

                    ✳

Readers in a police state
search lines for the hidden
                    forbidden

& Russian critics used their reviews

                                    of books and plays
              to criticize the culture

              and writers could be demonized
              for not being "useful" enough
              not enough on the line
                            for social change

              & for not overtly opposing
                            the demons of the
                                    police state.

                 A writer is never right enough
                 for the right
                 nor left enough for the left

                              *

Famous Words from Oct. o' '88

"The people I fear are those who look for
 a particular program
 between the lines and are determined
 to see me as either liberal
                    or conservative.
 I am neither liberal, nor conservative,
 nor gradualist, nor monk, nor indifferentist.
 I should like to be a free artist and nothing else,
 and I regret God has not given me the strength
 to be one.

 I hate lies and violence in all their forms....
 Pharisaism, dull-wittedness, and tyranny
                    reign not only in merchants' homes
 and police stations—

 I see them in science, in literature,
                    among the younger generation.
 That is why I cultivate no particular predilection

for policemen, butchers, scientists, writers,
                    or the younger generation.

I look upon tags and labels as prejudices.
My holy of holies is the human body,
            health, intelligence, talent, inspiration, love,

and the most absolute freedom imaginable,
freedom from violence and lies."

                    *

            Chorus of Critics:

Tell us your views   take a stance
Take a stance take a stance

            Chekhov:

simplicity
        sincerity
precise
        and non-slop descriptions
combined with "nonintervention"
by the author

because the author
by stating his/her
solution to
        to the problem
is taking unfair
                advantage
                    of the reader

Th' reader must
draw its own conclusions
based on the evidence
with complete freedom

                    *

Two Interesting Events

At the end of the year
      the Pushkin Prize
            from the Academy of Sciences
                to Chekhov
        for his collection, *At Twilight*

and in the kitchen of
        his family's house,
      Lenin at 18 first read Marx.

33

The Year of the Wood Demon:
(1889)

February

The revised version of *Ivanov*
        at the Alexandrinsky Theater in Petersburg.

Chekhov made last minute changes
      and the famous lead actor
            threatened to quit

      —Aeschylus Aeschylus—

It was a triumph of whacked palms
Chekhov joined the actors on stage
      his legs feeling weak and buckly
           his ticker tick-pounding

      in the ego-bronze
      of tossed flowers
      and weeping fans

      *

In March, '89
Chekhov wrote to Suvorin,
"Guess what, I'm writing a novel!!!
And what an intricate plot!
        I've called it
        Stories from the Lives of My Friends."

                    *

By late winter the
        novel was taking up all his time
This was when he wrote his friend Anna Yevreinova
"Oh, what a novel!
If it were not for the cursèd censorship,
I'd promise it to you in November.
There's nothing in the book
inciting anyone to revolution
but the censors will
                ruin it anyway.
Half the characters say,
            'I do not believe in God,'
and there is a father
whose son
        has been sentenced to life at hard labor
        for armed struggle."

By the end of '89
    Chekhov felt it
        would never pass the censor
            & decided to destroy the manuscript—

        or did he?
        Time to look for it in the post-Sov
        archives

                    *

Also in March, '89
his older brother Nikolai, nicknamed Kolya,

118

described in the Chekhov literature as a
painter with many unfinished canvases
& a grumpy alcoholic,
came down with typhus.
Chekhov cured him, but discovered
                what they call "galloping consumption"

For the second straight spring and summer
                Chekhov rented a house
                for his family in the Ukraine

He brought Nikolai with him
but his brother wasted quickly, sleeping in a chair

                        *

May 4

        "Last night
        I remembered I'd promised
        a farce for the actor Konstantin Varlamov

        Today I wrote it
                A Tragedian in Spite of Himself
        and I've already sent it off."

                        *

        Chekhov tended to his brother
                        till mid-June

        when his older brother Alexander
                        arrived to replace him

        & he went away with friends
                        for a five-day rest.

        "Never in my life shall I forget
                the muddy road, the grey sky,

the tears on the trees"

when in the morning
a peasant came from the town
with a wet telegram,
                    "Nikolai is dead."

It was the first time
the Chekhov family
            had seen a coffin in their house.

                    *

Later in the summer
he went to Odessa

and then to Yalta
            in the hot south

wrote a major tale,
            "A Dreary Story,"

which shook up the critics
who had long begun
            to assemble in smile-snarls
                        looking for Chekhov to fall

During this
            he finished *The Wood Demon*

            It had begun as a collaboration
            between Chekhov and Suvorin

            but after one scene Suvorin lost interest
            and Anton continued it.

On October 5, Chekhov submitted it to the censor.
and then an "unofficial theatrical committee"
            of three liberal professors

convened in St. Pete
to determine whether
    The Wood Demon

was suitable for production
at the gov't-run Imperial Theater

Tough luck, Anton

They decreed that *The Wood Demon*
  was a
      "beautiful dramatized novel,
      unsuitable for the stage."

*

Never Give Up—Part II

Chekhov
immediately reworked it
and the Abramov Theater in Moscow
put it on,
with an opening night of 12-27-'89.

*

The hero of *The Wood Demon*
is a doctor who vehemently
tries to save forests and wild species
      from stupid destruction

—Chekhov constantly mentioned
    the degradation of the environment,
      excessive clearcutting,
        river-fouling and illness
      from industrial pollution
          in his works

(see, for instance, "The Steppe," or "In the Ravine")

In *The Wood Demon* the doctor gives
a speech
      that might in our era have
      been delivered at a convention
            of the Sierra Club:

"The timberlands of Russia
         are moaning beneath the ax
Billions die
The habitat of birds and animals
           are destroyed
Rivers go shallow and dry up
They shapes of landforms
        are gone forever
The climate devastated
        and each day finds the earth
        more poor and ugly."

              *

The critics devoured the play
        down to the spine
and Chekhov withdrew it
        from his works.

              *

Never Give Up—Part III

During th' next few seasons
    he reworked it very much,
        and it appeared eight years later
            as *Uncle Vanya.*

              *

    It's all batter
    for the Divine Waffle

              *

The Hovering Minus Sign

Chekhov was feeling
        down down down
                at year's end '89

In January he was turning thirty
    The failure of his play
        The death of his brother
He distrusted his own work
It was so hasty

"As a writer I'm a complete ignoramus"
           he wrote to Alexei Suvorin.

        Around that time
        he chanced upon some notes
        his brother Mikhail had taken at a criminal law
        course.

    It made him meditate about prisons:
   "We focus all our thought on the
                criminal BEFORE his sentence
   is given. Then, once in prison,
   we pay no attention at all.

          WHAT HAPPENS IN PRISON?"

(It sounds like the million-prisoner USA of the '90s.)

    He decided to travel to a distant penal colony,
    bleak and recently acquired,
    on the island of Sakhalin
             in the Pacific just north of Japan

   where convict-colonizers
          were sent

        and write what he saw.

He would escape the
blasts of bitter-shitter critics
(and the relentless pressure
            of his era
               on writers
                     to "be useful")

and go where suffering and injustice
                     were touchable

                  ✳

Not many cared.
The subject of prison colonies
                  in 1890
was about as popular
            as, say, discussing
waste reduction in a big U.S. city
                  in 1990

"The much glorified 1860s
                  did NOTHING
                        for the sick
   and the people in prison,"
                  he wrote to Suvorin

                  ✳

Research Methods

Chekhov researched in St. Petersburg,
compiling 65 books—
            penology, history of Sakhalin's colonization,
            the island's native people, memoirs of travelers,
            wildlife and natural resources.

                  ✳

Chekhov met with the head
of the National Prison Administration,
who immediately wrote to the director
                of the prison at Sakhalin
to keep Chekhov from interviewing political prisoners.

*

Back in Moscow
        his sister Maria
                and her student friends
                        at the women's teachers' college

were his research assistants
looking up articles in periodicals
and translating from languages he couldn't read

*

Suvorin gave him a 1,500 ruble advance
        for a series
                he would write
                        for *Novoya Vremya*
called "Travels Across Siberia"

34

1890

His sixth book of stories,
Morose People,
dedicated to his friend Tchaikovsky.

*

That late winter or spring o' '90 were
        student demonstrations—
        they wanted autonomy for the university

the admission of Jews & women without quotas
the lowering of tuition
and the ending of police surveillance.

There were fights with the Cossacks
                              arbitrary arrests

Chekhov followed the dems
          picked up a leaflet
                    and wrote the demands
to his friend Suvorin,
          in a letter that shows Chekhov's
          struggle with anti-Semitism
                    and cynicogyny:

"I think the flames are being fanned most forcefully
by a bunch of young Jews and by the sex
that is dying to get into the university,
though five times worse prepared than the men,
while even the men are miserably prepared
and with rare exceptions make
                              abominable students."

∗

Sakhalin

The journey to Sakhalin
was 10,000 versts
          by train, boat, and back twisting coach

A verst is ca. 3,500 feet: so the trip was 6,629 miles.

∗

Gasping
          at the edge of
                    the huge Siberian plain.

Writing five articles for *Novoya Vremya*,
   as he paused to rest for a week
                  in Tomsk, Siberia.

*

July 9, Chekhov
      journeyed through the Tatar straights

viewing the island of Sakhalin
                looming nigh

arrived on July 11

*

Sakhalin had five penal colonies.
There was an element of
          Hotel California about it—
You could check out
      but never leave

and so when a prisoner served his/her time,
                he/she had to remain as a settler

*

The military governor
      allowed him access to the archives
and to talk to all
          but the political prisoners

*

He drew up a 13-point questionnaire
                for the residents
    and had the local print shop print it

Every morning at 5 AM he began his
rounds to question the prisoners.

He compiled a census on 10,000 convicts & settlers

He saw daily beatings

& convicts chained to wheelbarrows
             slaving on their stomachs
                          in the mines

*

The Barrows of Evil

"I had conversations with convicts
                 handcuffed to wheelbarrows."

*

He asked to view a lashing

The prisoner had been sentenced to 90 blows
A doctor took a look
        to see if the whipee could stand all 90

Other convicts
        milled around the whip zone
while the victim was strapped
                          to the bench

128

A guard counted off the lashes
                    "1, 2, 3......"
in a hellcalm chant

The whipper whipped five times on one side
then waited thirty seconds

walked to the other side of the victim
                        and whipped five more

The victim screamed
his nakedness swelling in red-blue welts
                        of pain-skin

He shouted for mercy, then screamed, then vomited
                then moaned & rasp-gasped
                            & no more words

For nights it swirled in Chekhov's sleep:
"I dreamed of the torturer
            and the disgusting whipping-bench."

                    *

All women practiced prostitution
The guards reserved
            the youngest and prettiest
                        for themselves
Parents sold their daughters

"I saw starving children,
I saw thirteen-year-old kept women,
and pregnant fifteen-year-olds.
Girls start practicing prostitution at the age of 12,
sometimes before the start of menstruation."

                    *

In the book he was to write
the fiercest words were against the
colonial violence of the convict settlers

who were exterminating the indigenous
Gilyak and Ainu people in Sakhalin

                              *

He spent exactly two months
          on Sakhalin
                    and had enough research
completed
to bring a message of prison reform

He thought of visiting the
United States
          before returning to Moscow
                    but couldn't afford it

He came home by boat
                    south on the Tatar Straights
through the
          Sea of Japan
                    past Vladivostok

     past Korea,
          through the Korean Straits
                    to Hong Kong.
Then
uh-oh, a typhoon,
          so mortally whirly-swirly
the captain told him
          to keep a pistol handy
for self-shoot
          if the ship went down
                    in the shark-swarmed
                              South China Sea.

The Fates
          snipped not his
                    golden threads

and he steamed past Vietnam
to Singapore, and up the

Straits of Malacca
past Sumatra to Ceylon/Sri Lanka
where he had
some wild hours
in a coconut grove
one night
with a dark-eyed damsel

he could brag about
among males
back in Moscow.

From Sri Lanka
up the Red Sea through
the Suez Canal

up past Mt. Sinai,
past the glory of Ionia
up the Bosporus
past Constantinople
to the Black Sea
to dock at Odessa
at the mouth of the Dniester

on 12–1-'90
a voyage of 2 months.

＊

Chant Against Torture and Cruel Punishment

Chekhov:

"It may be pointed out
relevantly
that jurists and penologists
consider corporal punishment to include more
than beating with fists or birch rods

It also includes shackling, the 'cold' treatment,
the schoolboy 'no dinner,' 'bread and water,' prolonged
kneeling, repeated touching of the forehead to the ground,
and binding the arms.

This inventory has made me suffer.

Corporal punishment has a
bad effect on physical health."

*

It took Chekhov five years
amidst his medical practice,
       the crafting of tales,
            and a bewilderingly complicated
        life as a scientist, bon vivant
           and a person
              keeping up contacts

to turn out his book on Sakhalin

*

He did not
      investigate
          the dungeons of
              Schusselburg fortress

   where so many
     political prisoners
        died or went insane.

*

Whis... Whis... Whisper

The trip to Sakhalin
      seemed to displease

the big city
intelligentsia

They whispered he was dried up
Lost his chops
That he was just a product
of the right wing nut
Alexei Suvorin

That he needed
those distant convicts
to find some facts

to stir his dried-out dearth

35

1891

In January, he went to St. Petersburg, but was
depressed and put off by the geekiness
of the hungry-for-others'-failure of the literati.

It was then he wrote,
"Were I to shoot myself, it would afford great pleasure
to nine-tenths of my friends and admirers."

＊

As if to defy the whisperers
in March of '91
he went to Western Europe
for the first time

with Alexei Suvorin.

Vienna, then Venice, Rome, and Naples

＊

It's all Material for Short Stories

"I rode horseback to
                    the foot of Vesuvius
It was so rough
I felt as if I'd been to the secret police
                    and been flogged!

What a torture to climb Vesuvius
  Mountains of lava
        congealed waves of molten minerals
You take one step forward
            and fall a half step back
    sometimes in ashes up to the knees!

Two and a half hours it took!
You're ashamed to turn back
            for fear of ridicule
I stood at the edge of the crater
and looked down into it
        as if I were looking into a teacup
The surrounding earth
        is covered with a thick
        coating of sulphur
            and gives off a dense vapor

Sparks and red-hot rocks fly everywhere
and smoke pours out of the crater,
while Satan lies snoring beneath the smoke.

I now believe in hell
The lava is so hot
        that a copper coin
            will melt in it"

                    ✳

Then Nice, then Paris—saw the Paris World Exposition
and the Eiffel Tower
        and back to Moscow, May 2.

134

*

Pogroms of '91

The tsar's anti-Semitic uncle
became governor-general of Moscow
and all 30,000 Jews were brutally expelled
on the first day of Passover

The sick were moved on stretchers.

This happened in other Russian cities
            and I've not found a word about it
                        in Chekhov's letters

*

Vladimir Ilyich Lenin
            was living "under restrictions"
in Samara, 1,000 miles away from St. Petersburg

but his mother, who had pull,
convinced officialdom
            to let him take the law exams
                        in St. Petersburg

In the fall of '91, he passed the bar exams with honors
and was admitted to the bar.

He opened a law practice
in his home city in Samara, Simbirsk
and worked with the poorest people.

*

Up at dawn
Made some coffee
wrote at a windowsill
            not a desk

At 11
    he went out
        to pick mushrooms
Lunch at 1
    then a nap
then to write
        till evening
Chekhov's schedule
the summer of '91

deep in debt
    from a year of travel

36

Bad Harvests

'Tween '91 and '14
there were 12 bad harvests
soil was exhausted
even the Black Earth region of the Ukraine

Two straight years
'90-'91 and '91-'92
there were full-scale famines.

Because of Russia's expansionist foreign policy,
the gov't encouraged export of grains
It needed the foreign exchange
to pay its foreign debt.

Hungry stomachs
Slithery borders.

*

Some of the peasants
were so psychologically demonic

that during the famine
        they invaded the towns along the Volga

trashing hospitals and attacking the doctors
who had come to fight the cholera epidemic, whom
the mouziks accused of poisoning their wells.

*

Lenin on Famine

At twenty-four, the utterly obsessed Lenin
already looked old, bald and scorch-faced.

When the peasants gathered in the city where Lenin lived,
a committee was formed to help the hungry.

He had the same weakness
                as other leftists
in viewing the famine as a goad for the growth of
the urban proletariat:

      "The famine is the direct consquence
      of a particular order.
      So long as that order exists,
      famines are inevitable."

*

      The police state feared riots
      and censored
              newspaper accounts
      of the hunger

      It forbade private collections
              for the victims
      Only the Red Cross and the Church
              were allowed to help

Tolstoy
    defied them,
        collected large sums
and with his daughters
    set up 100s of soup kitchens

                    *

Chekhov followed Tolstoy

The peasants were eating the horses
that would have pulled their plows
                        the upcoming spring
or selling them for nothing.
His plan was to purchase horses
in the provinces
        East of Moscow,
fatten them over the winter
then give them to the peasants
                in time for planting.

He placed ads in journals
wrote 100s of letters to friends
    and gathered rubles
                    from rich landowners

                    *

    During famines the peasants
    would strip the thatch
        from their roofs
                to feed livestock

*

And in his mode
      of knowing for himself
he traveled twice
in the cold, dread winter
         to the provinces

helping to distribute
      grain, coal and portable stoves

Don't kill your horses
      he went by sleigh
Don't sell your horses
      by sleigh by sleigh
in the utter cold
      village to village
One night he was lost in a snowstorm
      and risked getting buried

37

Melikhovo

Because of his fame
        his time-track was spilling
                with admirers & sightseers
He was feeling "rickety"
He HAD to get out of Moscow

so in February of '92
        the winter of the famine
he purchased an estate
near the village of Melikhovo
                two hours from Moscow

It had a ten-room one-story house
on 575 acres
        250 of which were forests
        with two ponds

The price was 13,000 rubles
                His friend Suvorin advanced
                him 5,000 and co-signed
                the mortgage

*

Even in the 19th Century There Were Hideous Closing Costs

It cost about
1,000 rubles
in various
        scam-fees

(sounds like our own era)

to get past the greed-heads
and own Melikhovo

*

At the age of 32
        the boy from Taganrog
                with snow-soggy shoes—
The grandson of serfs
        an estate!

A gift from his memory lobes
                his language lobes
vast vim
        & flowin' ink!

*

Few things more thrilling
than watching great Gaia shoot green
                through melting snow
                        in a new country home

working on the hotbeds
building starling houses
hanging curtains
moving curtains
digging a well
patching the roof
cementing the stove tiles
repairing fences and sheds
and installing an indoor toilet!

*

He planted 80 apple trees, 60 cherries
and firs and elms,
        rose and lilac bushes.

"We have sowed 38 acres of rye

I busy myself with the orchard
Such a wealth of raspberries and strawberries!
Many plum and apple trees

The best thing is our alley of lindens."

*

In years to come
a reputation
among the locals
for a way
       with roses

*

Dialogue

Stare at the pond's edge
             for an hour or two

mark out new paths through the woods
go horseback riding
loving the smell of fresh mown hay

then head to his study
       to work on "The Grasshopper."

*

The slight
"thwocking" sound
of mushrooms being plucked
       and arranged
       in a wicker basket

in the woods
after a rain

*

Maria's narrow room
            at Melikhovo
with a large photo
of her brother
            above the bed

                    *

She hated being away from him
She was his confidante
    A tireless researcher & letter writer
        Did the accounts
            Protected his privacy
                Gave up marriage

                    *

Love of Houseguests

The family loved the action
                    from fame

His mother Yevgenia
                    spent much of her time cooking
His father stayed out of the way
                    but kept a log of guests

Ahh the mooches and visitors!
Painters, poets, young women
                    with manuscripts,
brothers with children, local doctors,
playwrights, editors buzzing for Gaia

Guests slept four to a room
            they snored in the hallways
            or any available prone-zone
            throughout the house.

                    *

Trying to finish "Ward #6"
on Easter weekend '92
with the ink-addling aura of guests
and "I haven't
            gotten a single line written!"

*

The Woodcock

One of the houseguests
was the landscape painter Isaac Levitan
a friend of Chekhov
            from his days at the university

Russian men loved to
            traipsed in the copse
                        with guns
to give little animals
            some lead

So it was on a fine spring day
      in Melikhovo
            —April 18, '92—
                  such a famous day
as to be a gnomic warning
to be careful around
            minds great or small
—you'll wind up in their books and plays!

Levitan shot at a bird
            which fell wounded
                  by his feet

"It had a long beak, large dark eyes,
  and fine plumage."

It looked at the painter and writer
                  with astonishment

Levitan closed his eyes
            and begged Doctor Chekhov,

"Kill it."

"I can't."

The bird continued its stunned stare.
Finally Chekhov killed it.

"One lovely, amorous creature less,"
            he wrote,
"and two imbeciles went back home
                        and sat down to table."

                    *

Wait a Minute, I'm in Your Story!

Just a few days after the shooting
a literary bitter-buzz
came out of Moscow
over Chekhov's latest story,
            "The Grasshopper,"

Isaac Levitan was having an affair
with Sofia Kuvchinnikova
        the wife of a doctor
                friend of Chekhov

and Levitan saw himself
limned in "The Grasshopper"
as the cynical, leching painter
whom the wife of a doctor was balling

Levitan severed with Chekhov
and contemplated a
                Pushkinian duel challenge
and Sofia Kuvchinnikova

reproached her husband's friend
for the ink

"I was in Moscow yesterday,"
Anton wrote on April 29,
"and almost smothered there
from boredom and all kinds of reproach

An acquaintance of mine, a woman of 42,
has recognized herself in the 20 year old heroine
of my story

and all Moscow is accusing me of libel."

Chekhov stood firm in the
adage of ink:
"hang with me
hang in my stories"

*

Vladimir Lenin
was 22 when he read
"Ward #6"
(the last story Chekhov
published in Suvorin's *Novoya Vremya*)

& it gave the future leader of Russia
an attack of "genuine anxiety....
I could no longer
stay in my room
I stood up & went outside.
I felt that I myself
was locked up
in Ward #6."

38

Femina Femina

Women fall for Chekhov
Even in 1996
       a hundred years later
He's viewed as one of the most fair
most sensitive
     and for a man just about
     the best scope on the
         women of 19th century Russia

& a century ago
they came to Melikhovo
the lissome damozels of '92-'95
       to visit the fatal genius

Some were stunned by his writing
Others were attracted by his style of living
Some came to the household
      as friends of his sister Maria

Some were writers themselves
      hoping to join a precious circle

Many were stunners
      what Balzac called "stingrays"
and were exquisitely beautiful.

           *

In '91 to Suvorin
  "In women
    I like beauty
      most of all"

He wanted them gay, witty
                and full of élan

but hesitated
        to "fall" in love.

Pretty women surrounded him
                in love, in secret love
                        or prone to love

*

Year after year,
        say from 1892 through '96
he aloofed himself
from those in love with him

using some love-dodge ploys
in his letters
more brilliant than Ovid's
                Ars Amatoria

*

He was,
in current parlance,
        "afraid to commit"

*

He had a male perception
of women as voracious grabbers:

"Women grab men's youth,
but not mine"
        he wrote to Alexei Suvorin

*

Through his sister
        he met an 18-year-old teaching assistant

148

at the school where Maria taught:
Lika Mizinova

She was beautiful,
        and had a fine singing voice.

Chekhov and Lika Mizinova
        had met before he went to Sakhalin
        back in '90

and he invited her to Melikhovo
that first spring.

In his letters to her, ordinarily
        very cagy and tinged with aloofness
lines of need spun through:
"I'm looking forward to seeing you,
dreaming of your arrival
        as a Bedouin in the desert
                dreams for water."

and, "I miss you. I'd give five rubles for a chance
                to speak to you, if only for five minutes."

∗

Lydia Yavorskaya

Another visitor that summer was the actress
                Lydia Yavorskaya
Henri Troyat says Yavorskaya
        was "young and sinuous"
                with "flirtatious ways"

She was an "exquisitely beautiful blonde"
wrote exceptional Chekhov scholar Simon Karlinsky

∗

Tatyana Shchepkina-Kupernik

And then there was the
stunning teen-age perf-poet
    Tatyana Shchepkina-Kupernik
who showed up on the scene
        in the early '90s

Karlinsky avers there were
      low standards in Russian poetry
           that she wrote trite doggerel

      but three of her comedies had been produced
              at the Maly and Korsh Theaters
              by the time she was 20

Karlinsky says she formed with
         her friend Lydia Yavorskaya
a kind of a sexual freedom league
and that they balled
      both Chekhov and Suvorin

                 *

Pushy stunners
      are barrier-breakers
It was Kupernik
    who three years later
helped patch up
        Chekhov's quarrel
        with the painter Levitan

                 *

And then there was the tiny, raven-tressed, elegant
and married writer Lydia Avilova
         who fell for Mr. Aloof too
      chased him for years
           & wrote a book about it

                 *

Plus also the "ravishing Ukrainian actress"
Maria Zankovetskaya
       with whom he spent time in early '93
       told her he'd write a play for her,
           sure, Anton, sure
  spent a night with her drinking champagne,
     and they toboganned together
          down an icy hill near St. Petersburg

*

     And others
     You can find them
         in the archives

39

A Hunger to Cure

> an actual earth of value to
> construct one....
> —Charles Olson

The peasants lined up at dawn
from as far as 25 miles from Melikhovo

He saw them for free
giving out free the medications brought from Moscow

*

July Cholera Epidemic
(1892)

He was the medical supervisor
       of the district around Melikhovo
to fight the oncoming cholera

151

He gave free treatment
                    to over 1,000 peasants
                            that summer

Stopped writing, to heal.

*

Cholera

An acute, watery diarrheal disease
caused by *Vibrio cholerae*
anaerobic bacteria
            that grow "on relatively
                        simple media"

Fluid loss may be extreme
exceeding one liter per hour

Cholera
    in epidemics
            is mainly waterborne
from voluminous liquid stools
            soaking the clothing and linens

The setting for epidemics
            is extreme poverty
                    & lack of pure water

It can kill
    you in 4–6 hours

sunken eyes, hoarse voice,
        thirst, faint heart sounds,
    severe muscle cramps

*

I am Utterly Alone

(the summer of '92)

Chekhov:

"We district doctors are prepared; we have a definite plan of action, and there is every reason to believe that we will also decrease the percentage of cholera deaths in our regions. We are without assistants; we will have to be doctors and attendants at one and the same time. The peasants are crude, unsanitary and mistrustful, but the thought that our labors will not be in vain makes it all almost unnoticeable.

> Of all the Serpukhov doctors
>> I am the most pitiful,
>>> my carriage and horses are mangy,

> I don't know the roads,
>> I can't see anything at night,
>>> I have no money,

> I tire very quickly,
>> and most of all—I can't forget
>>> that I ought to be writing....

I am completely and utterly alone."

∗

The fall of '92 the epidemic ebbed.

∗

Chekhov: Cosmologist

"Perhaps the universe
is suspended on the

tooth of some
            monster."

40

Idti v Narod:
Not Just Talking About It
(1893–1896)

He supervised and planned the building of a local school
and later two more schools in
            neighboring villages the next 3 years

            collected books for libraries,
            including his hometown Taganrog
            to which he directed, o'er time,
                        1,000s of books

He talked local officials into building a local highway
and built for the locals a beautiful bell tower
                        for their church

            Doing it, not just talking theory
            Doing it not just talking

                        *

            Walking
            through the garden
            with his two dachhunds
                        Bromide & Quinine
            the summer of '93

                        *

The Writings of '93

"The Chorus Girl"
"Story of An Unknown Man"
"Sakhalin Island"
      (the latter published
      in six installments
      in *Russkaia Mysl*)

*

A famous young novelist
named Ignaty Potapenko
came to Melikhovo
        the summer o' '93

He played the violin
        and had a passable baritone
Lika Mizinova had a beautiful voice
& Chekhov liked to hear them
at the piano
singing the art songs
        of Glinka and Tchaikovsky

*

Fun in Five

In Moscow from Melikhovo
He met his women friends
      in room 5
        at the Grand Hotel

Lika, Lydia, Lydia, Tatyana
        and a couple of others

*

Thirty-three
& maybe slightly actress-batty
in *fin de siècle* Moscow

known
in his visits to Moscow that fall
                    for his partying:

"Never have I felt so free
            I have no apartment
                    so I live wherever I please
I still don't have a passport,
                    and ... girls girls girls."

                    *

In Nov. '93
        Lydia Yavorskaya signed one of her
        letters to him from Rome,
                    a measure of her flame:

"I miss you and love you.
                    Your Lydia."

        Yavorskaya later destroyed her
        letters from Chekhov
                        when she married
        a nobleman in late '96
        and became a Princess

                    *

Birth Control

Famous in his own time
        & a hundred years since
                for his ethical behavior
and as a doctor
Chekhov no doubt

knew what there was to know
about birth control

but there's nothing in the textbooks
about birth control techniques
in the randy late-19th century Russian theater

Actress and author interruptus
was an obvious possibility

and the literature says that
sheaths of sheep's-gut
were used

and by the 1880s the Germans
and perhaps the Dutch
had invented cervical caps

plus old remedies
for early miscarriage:
pennyroyal
or other herbal combinations.

The whole subject, then as now,
of private touching private:
risky, brisky, and tssk-tssky

✳

That fall Lika Mizinova
learned about her
hot rival Lydia Yavorskaya

and sent him
a mock-dread letter:

"Mme Yavorskaya spent the evening with us
She told us Chekhov was charming &
she wanted to marry him,
whatever it took,
& I promised to do all in my power

for your mutual happiness....

Write me a few lines
            to tell me whether
      you are in love with Lydia Yavorskaya—
Write them to me, of course,
                        and not to her!

Write, I beg you! "

                *

Chekhov aloofed himself
& just weeks later Lika
and Ignaty Potapenko
            began an affair

      Potapenko abandoned his wife and kids
      and traveled to Paris with Lika
      where soon she was pregnant

                *

Chekhov stored the affair
            for a later *œuvre*-insertion.

41

1894

      A cough cough
shakes the soul
      cough cough
tears the key from the latch
      cough cough
axes the life-roots
      cough cough
cuts thought

guts art

In February of '94
the cough was such a threat
though he tried to foist it off
                    as bronchitis

that he went south to the Crimea
like someone now
        might fly to Barbados
                    to shake the flu

                ✳

Had a small
        studio
            built behind the
                    Cherry Orchard

        to hide
        for ink-glide

He called it the "Oven" or his "Doll's House"
and there he wrote
"The Peasants,"
"The Story of an Unknown Man"
"Three Years," "Ariadne"
        and *The 'Gull*

                ✳

The Haystack-Eros Synapse

In one of his letters
almost a haiku
on the curves and smells
of fresh-tossed grass:

"Two hours on a haystack
& you'll think yourself
in the arms of a naked woman!"

*

In early fall
He made his second trip to the West
first to Yalta in the south, then over to Odessa
                    at the mouth of the Dniester River
to Vienna, to Abbazia on the Adriatic,
to Trieste, Venice, Milan, Genoa.

In Milan Chekhov visited a crematorium,
and, from youth a fan of
                    strolls in cemeteries
                looked forward to the
                upcoming walk through
                    th' thanatopolis in Genoa

            which made his travelmate Suvorin
            scratch notes in his diary
                    about his friend's morbid tastes

        but the author whose cough shook the life-roots
        and the Doctor long dyed with the dying
                        felt peace in the
                            sod towns of Gaia

*

Lika wrote him from Switzerland
7 months pregnant

Potapenko had gone with his wife to Italy

She begged Chekhov to detour through Zurich
but Chekhov wrote back he had to go to
Paris with Suvorin
            and then back to Melikhovo.

She too was
　　　cruising for an *œuvre*-insert

42

1895

The Island of Sakhalin: travel notes,
came out as a book in June.

✳

The censors that year
cut out a number of sections
that spoke about religion.
in his story, "Three Years,"
about the decline of a family
in the pond-culture business world of Moscow,

✳

In the summer, spitting blood.

✳

Maria was taking medical courses
　　　　to help her brother
　　　　　　with the peasants

✳

Tolstoy

August 8, 1895
Chekhov went to see Tolstoy
　　　at Yasnaya Polyana

They went skinny dipping in the river
and had their first chat
                    in the neck-deep current.

                    ✳

Lika visited Melikhovo
                    three times the summer of '95
                            after her baby had died.
In September he began *The Seagull*.
He finished the first draft in a month,
                    then re-scored weak sections.

                    ✳

Hey, I'm in Your Play!

                    There's always
                    that oh-no-ing dread
                    of a friend
                    scanning text
                    for
                    maskèd mention

                    ✳

December '95

In Lydia Yavorskaya's Moscow flat
            he read *The Seagull* to friends, and was shocked
            they believed it depicted Lika Mizinova's
            affair with Potapenko

            & that they i.d'd
            Potapenko's wife with Arkadina

                    ✳

In early 1896 he totally rewrote it.

*

One thing
Chekhov
        points out
                in *Th' 'Gull*:
there isn't
the same
        intoxicating praise
for Perf-Art
                in the country
as the city

*

Suvorin,
    seeing his pal
    scattered
    like a dropped
            bag of marbles
urged him to marry.

"I'm afraid of a wife
& a domestic routine
that will hamper me....
But, it's still better than
            bobbing on the life-sea
and tossing in the frail skiff of debauchery.

I don't care for mistresses anymore
& I'm gradually growing impotent with them."

*

Lenin

On December 20, '95
Lenin was arrested by the Okhrana

for conspiracy
        to publish a secret newspaper

The proofs of issue one were seized.

In the St. Petersburg prison
        he wrote pamphlets
                in invisible ink

*

inkwells
in
globs of
black bread,
swallowable

*

In '97 he
        was exiled three years to Siberia.

43

1896

The Coronation of a New Tsar
May

Alexander III passed on to the
        cosmic Kremlin
and for the coronation of his son
Nicholas II
a huge throng
was lured to a huge open space
        called Khodynka
near Moscow
for free food, trinkets and drink

2,000 were trampled to death
        in the grab-surge

Chekhov and Suvorin
        went to the cemetery
                to watch the victims' burial

The guy from Taganrog
startled in the red-eyed silence
        at the coffins of children

*

Good Works in '96

Urging local authorities to repair roads
urging for a telegraph and post office
urging to have a bridge rebuilt
urging to have a church rebuilt

and the new school at Talezh completed.

He organized fundraising efforts, concerts, and
        amateur theatrical productions to finance it

he drew up the plans for the school, bought the construction
        materials, supervised the carpenters and masons.
        The school opened in August o' '96
        priests blessed the walls
        the peasants gave Chekhov an ikon
           several loaves of bread,
                and silver saltshakers.

*

July 27, '96, diary:
"In the editorial offices
        of *Russian Thought*—
                bugs in the sofa"

*

In July of '96
        submitted *The Seagull*
                to the censors in St. Petersburg.

*

He'd written it for the Alexandrinsky Theater
in St. Pete,
        site of the '89 triumph of *Ivanov*

The very great actress
        Vera Kommissarzhevskaya
                at the beginning of her career
                stepped forth to play
                the role of Nina

*

He was moved to tears
at one of the rehearsals

*

There was the exhaustion from new rounds of blood-spit.
He still refused to learn from other doctors what it was.

44

The Premiere of the Sea Gull
(10-17-96)

The first performance of *The Seagull*
found Chekhov enmeshed
                in the Theory of Fluff

He allowed it to be a benefit

for a comic actress friend
and the audience was packed
with the partisans of
                    Overt Ha-Ha.

In the middle of the first act
ebullient drama critics
                    and journalists
leaped from their seats
                         and lunged for the bar

where they toasted one another,
"He's through"

        "He's written himself dry."

            "No, no, no, on the contrary,
                         it's all so watery."

"Whatever—the sign is on his
                    window: No talent Here"

            Sudden Hatred
            Clink Clink
            Sip   Sip
            Sudden Hatred

Malevolent literati, he once wrote,
are "not people,
        they're some kind of walking mildew."

At last,
      ah at long last
            they could demonize the too-famous Doctor—
Lines at the bar,
and lines of ink as the bars of a jail
            to sentence the criminal playwright
                         to the Lost Lethe of Losers

                    *

It was one of the more famous
of hiss-&-boo nights
such as those that greeted
The Rite of Spring, Carmen,
La Traviata, Aeschylus' *Archers*
or Dylan's electric guitar.

✳

When Vera Kommissarzhevskaya
began intoning Nina's
       play within a play

there was a spew of laughter
                then boos.

The sibilant component of
             applausamento-hissing
filled the theater
      with a million cobras
          at the end of Act One

& when the Act Three curtain came down
the ire-fire had engulfed the souls of the room
          & the mildew moaned with glee.

Chekhov went to a restaurant
        then walked walked walked
till he was exhausted.

"I roamed the streets
I sat
I kept thinking about the performance
I'll never allow another theater
         one of my plays
In theater, I'm doomed."

✳

The Humiliation of Perf

Chekhov's diary
for 10-17-96
is brisk & brief:
"Performance of my *Seagull*
at the Alexandrinsky Theater.
It was not a success."

$*$

One thing about the
        humiliation of trashed perf,
it did not prevent the genius
from trying to save
        a medical journal called
                        The Surgical Chronicle

It was going to fold
and was, said Chekhov,
        "an absolutely indispensable journal."

"I promised
        to find them a publisher,"
                        he wrote
"I searched
 I begged
 I humiliated myself
 I drove here and there
 I had dinner with the damnedest people
 but I found no one—
 If I weren't building the school
            which will cost me about 1,500
 I'd do the pub
        at my own expense"

                He finally lined up the $
                but there was trouble
                getting the authorities
                to approve the editor

45

Census Till Sick
(early '97)

Chekhov took part in the first national census
                              ever conducted in Russia
He traveled around the countryside
Supervising a group of other census takers
putting together the final report

*

February 19, 1897

There was a grand dinner
at the Continental
for the 35th anniversary
                  of the Emancipation

described in his diary:

"To dine, drink champagne,
                  make a racket
& give speeches on national consciousness,
                  the conscience of the people,
freedom, and the like,
while slaves in tail coats
            are running around your tables,
            veritable serfs, and your coachmen
            wait outside in the street,
                              in the bitter cold,
            this is lying to the Holy Ghost."

*

Early march
he was helping the *Zemstvo* in
Melikhovo
    build a school

                    *

The Attack in the Hermitage
(March 22, 1897)

In the ritzy restaurant
        called The Hermitage
                    with Suvorin
he opened his mouth to speak
            during the first course
& the blood started pouring from his mouth
A flow of shame to his cheeks
            when ice could not
                stop the flow
                    from his lips

Crystal decor
        perfect cuisine
                napkins of blood

& a shy playwright
who did not want to make a scene.

                    *

    Once the blood-spits began
    they persisted
                for weeks
    as he tried to heal
            the ink-killing coughs

        Chekhov:

"I must subject myself
                to various deprivations.
Can't leave the house after 3
Can't drink, or eat anything hot.

Can't walk fast
It annoys me
and puts me to anger

I cough. I cough. I cough
and so far,
it slowly subsides

                and I survive once again."

                        *

For the first time
he had to admit
he had tuberculosis

                        *

Blood and Ink

In the TB clinic
after the Hermitage attack
he corrected the
proofs of
        "The Peasants"

                        *

"The Peasants"
  had a difficult time passing
                        the creepy censors
They cut a number of sections—

Any way of going into

172

the post-Soviet archives
        and restoring those cuts?

*

"The Peasants" appeared in *Russian Thought*
    created a lit-storm. The Narodniki and Tolstoyans
    complained he was showing the
                sacred peasants
                        in a bad view

*

        After the hemorrhea,
                the doctors told him
        he'd have to give up medicine
                & live three-quarters of the year
        in a warm climate:
                the Crimea or the Riviera

*

    In September he left Russia for
    Nice on the Riviera
                where he stayed till the following spring

*

            Chekhov's Diary
            11-15-'97

            Monte Carlo
            I saw
            how the croupier
            stole
            a louis d'or

46

J'Accuse

On January 1, 1898 Émile Zola
published his famous "J'Accuse"
                                in *L'Aurore*

a letter to the president of France
tracing the conspiracy that had framed
Captain Alfred Dreyfus and later which
                                acquitted the evil Esterhazy

Chekhov read "J'Accuse" in Nice
and followed the case closely

"On Zola's side is the entire European intelligentsia
    and opposed to him is everything that is vile
    and of doubtful character."
                    2-22-98

He asked Alexei Suvorin
to send him a banned Marxist paper
                    with an article by Maxim Gorky

    "I acquainted myself with the
     case by reading the stenographic
     reports, which are quite different from
     what you find in the papers, and Zola's
     stand is clear to me."

*

The Background

Alfred Dreyfus was a career military officer
on the General Staff of
            the French army
                    with the rank of Captain

In October of 1894 Dreyfus was arrested for
                selling military secrets to Germany

He was put on trial with faked evidence and on
Jan 4, 1895, condemned to life imprisonment
                and was "publically degraded"
            in a frenzied public arousal of
                                    hatred

            (Chekhov noted
            in a letter to Suvorin
            how Dreyfus during the
            Degradation Ritual behaved
        "like a decent, well-disciplined officer"
            and yet journalists on hand had shouted
            things like "Shut up, you Judas!"
                            at Dreyfus.)

Captain Dreyfus was taken in March
                to the Ile du Diable, French Guiana.

The right wing press went hate-crazed
                with tauntings of Jews

*

Dreyfus' family stood by him
and investigated the case
                proceeding carefully
for the anti-Semitics of France

175

had seized the era

Those who had conspired to frame Dreyfus
leaked forged letters
        Dreyfus was alleged to have
                        sent to foreign military attachés

and finally,
Dreyfus' family went public
Major Esterhazy in '97 was courtmartialed
                        for forging the documents
but in a trial held in secrecy he was acquitted

*

Chekhov to Suvorin 2-6-98:
        "Little by little people became convinced
        that Dreyfus had in fact been convicted
        on the basis of a secret document which
        had been shown neither to the defendent
        nor his attorney, and law abiding people
        saw in this a fundamental violation of
                                the law."

*

Zola on Trial

Zola wanted the government
to prosecute him for libel

It worked.
In February of '98,
two months after "J'Accuse"
there was a trial in Paris
                which flashed "a fierce flood of light"
                on the case

The army worked up a sweat to crush him

176

and Zola was found guilty
     sentenced to a year in prison
       & thrown
           from The Legion of Honor

He appealed. There was a second
trial in July and not waiting for the guilty verdict
Zola fled to England
      for a year

till he could return.

           Chekhov:

"In court Zola represents French common sense, and so the
French love him and are proud of him, although they applaud the
generals who, simple-minded as they are, frighten them first with
the honor of the army and then with the threat of war."

              ✷

       Following the
       Zola case
       Chekhov
       finally became
           fluent in French

              ✷

     Suvorin's *Novoya Vremya*
     kept running articles
           that those who offered proof
           of Dreyfus' innocence
           were in the pay of an
                "International Jewish Syndicate"

              ✷

     It's exasperating
         to have a close friend
            with a right wing mean streak

but Chekhov could not break
with the magnate,
        whose grandparents also were serfs,
who had first brought
        Chekhov to the world
                of big-time publishing
loaned him money to buy Melikhovo
though he had years ago
        stopped writing for *Novoya Vremya*.

✳

He wrote Suvorin a long letter
resembling a legal brief
        to convince him to change his views
but refused to go public against him
        when *New Times*
        went on and on and on
                against Zola.

He condemned Suvorin
in a letter to his brother Alexander
for vilifying Zola
        in *Novoya Vremya*

while serializing Zola's new novel
without paying royalties

✳

Aroused by Phantoms

The concept of an "International Jewish Syndicate"
had the support of the Russian government

For instance, "The Protocols of the Wise Men of Zion"
        has been traced
        to the Paris office of the Okhrana
        produced

by one Ratchkovsky,
chief of the Paris Station of the Okhrana
in the 1890s

The Okhrana's Protocols
            were being quoted in newspapers
in France
        right after Zola's *J'Accuse* was published.

            The people are aroused
            Aroused by spectres
            Aroused by lingering lies

Every kind of rumor
            was believed in police state Russia:
the Masons were trying to free Captain Dreyfus
or the ever-wheeling Kaiser Wilhelm,
a Syndicate of Rabbis, the Jesuits, them French guys,
or maybe
        that most evil of tendencies:
    the German-Jewish-Protestant-Freemason
                                Conspiracy.

Chekhov,
    a famous gardener
            knew what it really was:

    "An evil plant began
    growing in the soil of anti-Semitism
    in a soil stinking of the slaughter-house."

And Zola helped keep France
                from swerving to the evil of
                            50 years later:

"It is for the best people,"
                said Chekhov,
"always ahead of their nations,
            to be the first to sound the alarm."

                    ✳

Chekhov
        went to the place of action
    spent a month in Paris
    where he met Dreyfus' brother Mathieu.

47

Not Forgetting His Home Town

When Chekhov returned from France that spring
        he brought back for his home city of Taganrog
            a statue of Peter the Great by
                    the then famous Mark Antokolsky

and 300 or so books of classic French writers
            plus a big packet
                    on the Dreyfus case

            for the Taganrog library

                    *

That summer he decided to built another school
in Melikhovo, his third.

Meantime, he rented a hut,
        bought desks,
            hired a teacher

                    *

        And against doctors' orders
        resumed treating the peasants

    while writing a trio of tales,

    "Gooseberries," "A Hard Case" and
                "Concerning Love."

Meanwhile, Vladimir Nemirovich-Danchenko, a
left-leaning playwright
& drama teacher
and Konstantin Stanislavsky
a wealthy actor and producer
who also ran a factory
in Moscow where
gold and silver threads were
produced

formed forces
for a revolutionary new theater
first called The People's Theater
and soon The Moscow Art Theater

Nemirovich-Danchenko wrote Chekhov
begging to be allowed
to produce *The Seagull*
the theater's first season

Anton turned him down
but Danchenko kept writing
& volunteered to come to Melikhovo
to explain his production ideas

As then, as now
the pushiest producer produces

and Chekhov allowed it

(It was playing all over Russia anyway, and getting
rave reviews in places like Odessa and Kharkov

plus never forget
the hunger for
r's From r's

rubles from royalties)

48

Meeting Olga Knipper
(September, '98)

In early September he
went to Moscow
        on the way to Yalta

and attended rehearsals
        in the Aeschylus mode
                and offered suggestions.

(He urged Stanislavsky to
to get rid of the actor that
                was playing Trigorin, for instance)

In his role
        of "Inspector of Actresses"

he noticed 28 year old Olga Knipper
who was playing the role of Arkadina

Knipper had studied acting
at Vladimir Nemirovich-Danchenko's drama school
and soon to become one of the
                best known actresses.

Yes, he noticed the Arkadina,
but scantily,
        he was so upset over what
                they were doing to his play

as he sat in the back
of the chilly hall
                in an overcoat
coughing and touching his beard
the stage lit up by candles in cups

A few days later
Chekhov also watched Olga rehearsing in
Alexei Tolstoy's blank verse drama, *Tsar Fyodor*
          based on the life of Ivan the Terrible's son
               —Olga Knipper played the tsar's wife Irina

It was the first production of the Art Theater
with vastly lavish costumes

From the gloom her voice, her voice
          a *vox flammae* that thrilled the chill—

     "Irina, in my opinion, is superb.
     What a voice, what dignity, what feeling!"
     Chekhov wrote his friend Suvorin
     "If I remained in Moscow
     I would fall in love with
                         this Irina."

                    ✳

Moves South to Yalta

The next day he left for the Crimea
               He'd been coughing blood

Settled in a villa in the suburb of Yalta
He was to use Yalta
          as a healing, home base
                         the rest of his life

                    ✳

His father died in the fall
     and he decided to move
          his mother and sister

     to Yalta too

                    ✳

Success in the Sticks
(Oct 26, 1898)

"My *Uncle Vanya*
  is making the rounds
                of the provinces"
      he wrote his brother Mikhail,
  "and it's been successful everywhere
  You never know when
                you're going to win
  and when you're going to lose

  I'd had no hope at all
                in that play"

*

He was purchasing a plot of land
                next to a Tatar cemetery
outside of town
to have a house built

There was a baker nearby
and a market for food
and the woods in the fall
had chanterelles
            and butter-'shrooms

*

And bought for 2,000 rubles
a cottage 18 miles
away on a steep hillside
above the sea

*

Gorky
(Late '98)

In October young Maxim Gorky
sent him a letter and two volumes
            of his *Stories.*

and thus began
       a longlasting friendship

            ✳

Maria Chekhov
begged Stanislavsky and Nemirovich-Danchenko
to cancel the *Seagull*'s run

His health was not good
He'd not liked the rehearsals

          She was afraid a reprise of
          wolf pack journalism
                might kill him

but, according to Stanislavsky's memoirs,
the Art Theater was in a
          desperate fiscal position
          and very badly needed
          the *'Gull* box office.

December 17 it opened to
          huge success.

            ✳

In the Crimea
     Chekhov would
         have those maddening and
            weakening spells of coughing

Then he'd get back his energy.

Though theoretically no longer practicing
he saw patients, toured schools,

worked for the local Red Cross
and raised money for the
famine victims of Samara

49

Rubles from Marx
(1899)

Alexei Suvorin was supposed
to publish Anton's
Collected Works
and Chekhov
was miffed at
Suvorin's slowness

In January, Chekhov signed a deal giving
the publisher Adolf Marx the rights to all his publications,
past and future, except plays,
for 75,000 rubles

Tolstoy
set up the deal
because he thought
Chekhov's moral tales
would reach millions of Russians
by means of Marx's inexpensive editions.

*

His inner circle
all tsk-tsk'd the deal—

but he told them
he'd still be selling
his stories to magazines

and he'd reserved for himself
            all royalties from plays
and he was to received additional monies
for future books—
        200 rubles for each 16 pages
        he wrote the next five years
        though the TB drums gave him only time
                            for 9 more tales—

                        *

        Marx made back his money
                        the first printing
        but Chekhov
        refused to demand
                a new deal

        When some of the
        most famous authors of Russia
                including Bunin, Gorky and Andreyev
        put together a petition to Marx
        Chekhov wouldn't let them send it

                        *

        There was a payment schedule—
        and when the first money came
        he gave 5,000 rubles
                to build a school in Yalta
        & 1,000 to help brother Alexander
                            buy a house

                        *

Student riots spread from Petersburg throughout Russia,
and young people were thrown into jail
                    after violent fights with police.

Mounted police
            whacked youth-backs
                    with riding crops

And then the government banned any mention
of the riots in the press.

Universities were occupied by the police
and before students were allowed to return
        each had to prove his pro-tsarist politics

Alexei Suvorin drooled with support
                        of the government
and was reviled across Russia

Chekhov was asked to make a public statement for the students,
but, as always, was reticent—

though behind the scenes, in letters to Suvorin,
he criticized Suvorin's defense
of the indefensible government in *Novoya Vremya*.

✳

Chekhov wrote him

> "Grant freedom of the press
> & freedom of conscience
> & you will have the quiescence
> you so desire—
>
> True, it may not last too long,
> but it will at least be enough
>   for our lifetimes."

✳

> The author of so many
>   core-seething tales
> held to his faith
>   in Gradual Betterment:

✳

Chekhov's Hymn to Gradualism

February 22, 1899

"It's not the government's fault
 It's the intelligentsia's
 As long as our boys and girls are students
                they're honest and good
 but as soon as they have to grow up and
 stand on their own,
        all hope and Russia's hope
                        go up in smoke
 and all that's left
 is cottage-owning doctors, rapacious public officials
 and thieving engineers

 I have no faith in our intelligentsia
 They're hypocritical, dishonest, hysterical
 ill-bred and lazy

 Its oppressors emerge from its own midst.

 I see salvation in individuals scattered here and there,
                        all over Russia,
        whether intellectuals or peasants,
     for they're the ones who really matter,
                however few they are.

 No man is a prophet in his own country,
 and the individuals for whom I speak
 play an inconspicuous role in society.
 They do not dominate,
                yet their work is visible."

                    ✳

Health ever ebbing
        he kept up the constant work
                for the good

189

In the first 3 months of '99
he was appointed honorary chair of the local girls' school
started a drive to raise money
            for victims of famine in Samara Province
and was on a commission to celebrate the
centenary of the birth of Pushkin

                        *

            He had six months to get
            all his fiction ready
                        for Marx.

            He did not have copies of early stuff
            and could not recall
                        some of the plots and titles

            His brother Alexander helped
            and his friend Lydia Avilov

            Copyists were hired
            and exercize books were shipped to Yalta

            amidst which
                        were prizes of literature
                                though some were a
            shocking disgorgment of quickies and medschoolia

            "What gibberish!"
                        he wrote to Lydia
                                as he reworked some of them.

            By mid-May he'd sent Marx 400 tales
                        marking about half not for use
                        which were published from '99 to '02
                        in a ten volume *Collected Works*

                        *

During the winter,
            —how is not clear from the archives—

Olga Knipper grew close to Chekhov's sister

so that when he left Yalta for Moscow on April 10
he again crossed

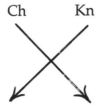

Ch   Kn

life-tracks
with with the dark-tressed actress.
Took her to an exhibit of
          Levitan's paintings
          Met her family.

50

Chekhov in Yalta
had not seen any performances
of *The Seagull's* sold out run

He asked Stanislavsky & Nemirovich-Danchenko
to view it

The season was over
& the scenery stored already in a barn

but the genius insisted
so a special perf
        at the Nikitsky Theater
was held for Chekhov & ten others

He invited Maxim Gorky to attend
but the police banned him from
coming to Moscow

The genius was very unimpressed
                    with the run-through
and wanted one actress dismissed
                    (not Olga Knipper)

& threatened to take the play away
                    from Stanislavsky.

He wrote Gorky,
    "The seagull herself
    gave such an abominable performance
    She blubbered very loudly through it all
    and the Trigorin strode
                    around the stage
                            speaking like a paralytic"

                    *

May 5, he gave Olga Knipper a picture of Melikhovo inscribed,
    "My house, where *The Seagull* was written.
    To Olga Leonardovna Knipper with best wishes."

When Chekhov returned to Melikhovo
                    from Yalta that month,
he asked her to visit
                    for the fruit flowers, the lindens
                            and the Japanese iris.

                    *

That May, Chekhov put Melkihovo up for sale at 25,000 rubles,
They packed to leave it for good,
                    mother and sister to Yalta.

                    *

In June of '99 Olga wrote that they meet in the south.
They agreed to rendezvous at Novorossiisk on July 18.
Then they went to Yalta
        where Chekhov's new house was under construction
        outside town at a place called Autka

*

She was all that he wanted at 39
Strong-willed
        keen for life
She had bundles of ardor and energy,
                and a love of newness
that shook with her lush, black hair—
She had abrupt mood changes—
She made him laugh—
She was, after all, a very good actress—
        & could be, on whim,
coquettish, dreamy, melancholic, dissatisfied—
Just what he wanted at 39.

*

August 2, Olga and Chekhov went to Moscow.
She had rehearsals
for the Art Theater's second season.

He had offered *Uncle Vanya* to the Maly Theater
but the Maly wanted changes in the script—
They couldn't allow, for instance, that a
Russian university professor
        should be fired at on stage

so he gave it to Nemirovich-Danchenko

*

He went to several rehearsals
where he heard again the soft chant
                "Aeschylus Aeschylus"
        set aside his shyness
        to intervene
        and chided
                both cast and director
                        when it seemed
        to wobble away from his plan.

193

Moscow grew chilly
      and grey with rain
and seizures of coughing
      drove him back to Yalta

*

"Cough cough cough
  Living with the concept that one must die
                is not pleasant at all
cough cough cough
but realizing that one will perish
      before one's time
is totally ridiculous"
      Chekhov told Gorky

*

The villa was done
and the family moved in on September 9

He planted many trees and shrubs
His garden up against
      the ancient Tatar cemetery

and a newfangled thing called a phone
with which
      he could call the author of
          War and Peace.

*

"In the Ravine,"
    one of this greatest
        was written in the fall
in his freshly plastered writing room
      with lily-of-the-valley wallpaper
          and a view of the sea

It spoke for all time
of the difficulty
        often the impossibility
of the weak but good
to protect and defend
                themselves
against those
        wielding the weapons
            of greed and selfishness

*

There were two gray
clip-winged cranes
            in the garden
who made waltzlike motions
and shrieks of joy
when the gardener
                came back from town.

*

Just about every day a
letter to Olga, dipped in his genius,
such as the one beginning:

"Dear wonderful actress!
Remarkable woman!
If you only knew what joy
            your letter gave me!
I make so low an obeisance
to you that
        my forehead touches
                the bottom of my well
which had been dug
to the depth of 55 feet!"

*

Uncle Vanya
had its premiere on October 26

at the Moscow Art Theater.

Chekhov:

It was the first time my so-called glory had kept me awake.

The telegrams started arriving in the night.
They awakened me to read them over and over on the phone
I kept running barefoot over the cold floor to the phone,
I got a bad chill.

Just when asleep, it would ring again.

But the next night I brought my slippers and
robe by the bed
and there were no telegrams
                              Such is fame

                    *

            What a season for the Art Theater!
            2,500 lined up for tickets the first day
            and many waited overnight.

51

Easing the Pain of Living
(November, 1899)

Doctors and families
kept shipping their
              sick penniless consumptives
                                    to Yalta

        Chekhov

They turn to me for help, and I'm at a loss
to know what to do

Narrator

Chekhov
raised
40,000 rubles
to open
a sanatorium
          in Yalta

The tuberculers
came up to him
beseeching, begging

like
the shades
          to Odysseus

Chekhov

It's so painful to watch their faces
as they beg, their pitiful blankets as they die

Narrator

The sanitorium was set up
and still exists
          bearing his name

52

1900

Chekhov and Tolstoy were elected
          honorary members
                    of the literary section
of the Academy of Sciences

early in the year.

Pining for Olga
Chekhov proposed that the Art Theater
tour the Crimea.
Stanislavsky finally agreed and
          Olga and Anton were together in early April.

Nemirovich-Danchenko and Stanislavsky
were starved for
          his new play

but Chekhov stalled
He wanted to see *Uncle Vanya*
so the trip to the Crimea fit both
          sets of desires

of Chekhov for Olga
and Nem/Stan for drama

The Art Theater by March of '00
had already paid Chekhov 3,500 rubles
in royalties for the *'Gull* and *Vanya*
and told him if he wanted more
they were willing to pay him 10% of gross receipts.

They came in a whole railroad car
singing songs
          and sending weird telegrams to friends
to the white sand
          and white houses
                    of Sevastopol

His mother Yevgenia
          put on her antique silk dress
                    to see a play by her boy

*

Olga Came to Yalta in July of '00

They met in Yalta again in July, till August 5.

Each night they kissed
                    in his study
she in her long white dress
            that showed off her curly erotic hair
She'd humm-sing Glinka's "Don't Tempt Me In Vain,"

They fucked
and whispered softly with
                    hands entwined

They tried to stay discreet
                    in the quiet house
with laughter & kisses & shussshes
            coffee and bread at midnight
            and then up the creaking staircase
                        to their separate rooms

✳

The Fascination Continued

Olga danced
herself
            short of breath
in a plunging neckline
                    the fall of '00

and wrote about it
            breathlessly to her
                    short-of-breath
                            playwright beau

✳

October 16,
      he finished the final dialogue
                for *The Three Sisters*
and hastened to Moscow
for a six-week stay at the Hotel Dresden

    There was a reading of
              the play
    in the Art Theater's lobby

    and when it was over
    there was a nervous silence
    the coughs of actors
             and toe-stare

    Some were not sure whether
    it was a tragedy or a comedy

    "It's not really a play yet,
        it's more of an outline,"
                someone said.

    Chekhov sulked away
    but rewrote much of the first
             two acts

             *

The early-hitting Moscow winter
drove him to Nice on the Riviera
in December

It was partly the lure of fleeing
that drove him,
      & partly the pressure of
          Three Sisters final revisions
& partly the lung-soothing clime.

From Nice to Florence and Rome
and then back to Yalta
        "to write and write."

On Dec. 24, 1900
Lenin and the Marxists
began *Iskra* (The Spark)

It was printed with small, crowded type
on onionskin
for easy smug/dist

and a secret network
was set up
to get it to readers
throughout the Russian empire

53

Olga Knipper and Marriage
(1901)

January 31, the premiere of *The Three Sisters*
at Moscow Art Theater.

*

On March 4, Cossacks charged students
in front of St. Petersburg's Kazan cathedral
lashing with their *nagaiki*
The students were protesting new laws
restricting academic freedom—

Gorky wrote Chekhov an eyewitness account:

Cossacks grabbed women by the hair
and whacked them with whips
They smashed into the protestors
in front of Petersburg's Kazan Cathedral
killed two

201

*

The night of the massacre
the Art Theater played
Ibsen's *Enemy of the People*
        in St. Petersburg
Stanislavsky expected instant arrests
Gov't censors sat in the audience
to make sure only the censored text was used.

"The audience was very excited,"
  wrote Stanislavsky,
"and answered even the slightest hints
  about liberty
      in every word
        of Stockman's protest."

*

  Royalties for the
  St. Petersburg's season o' '01
  for *Three Sisters* and *Seagull*:
      3,000 rubles!
        Sacred Russia!

*

At the end of March Olga
      came for ten days to Yalta
She was eager to get married
    and avoid the ritual
      of the creaking staircase

*

May 25, Olga and Anton were married
        in a church in Moscow.
He did not tell his sister or mom
They sent telegrams to their friends

then bride and groom took a train to the East
to visit Maxim Gorky for a day
            (under house arrest for
                taking part in the March demonstrations)

    then down the Volga
                to a sanitorium
                        for the in-vogue "Koumiss cure."

                    ✻

        Visits to what Skip James
                immortally sang as the
                            "Killing Floor"
        come even to great writers and actresses
        as when
            on their honeymoon
        they missed a steamer
                    at a place called Drunken Market
        and slept on the floor of a
        hut
                waiting for the whistle

                    ✻

Maria Chekhov viewed her brother's marriage
about as sourly
            as Dorothy Wordsworth

                    ✻

    Koumiss is fermented mare's milk
    from the people of the steppes
                who made it from camel's milk

    For a month he drank four bottles a day
                and stopped coughing almost entirely

    then they returned to Yalta.

    Olga went to Moscow in the early fall for rehearsals

and a time-sparged modern marriage

She was already
            one of the era's most famous.

Actresses in Russia
were treated to Total Adoration—
Audiences that wept actual tears
and twenty minute curtain calls

She loved it
She could not give up the thrill

"I am not young enough
            to shatter
                        in one second
    what it has taken me such pains
                        to achieve."

                    *

"If you and I
            cannot live together,"
                        he wrote her
"it is neither you nor I
    who are guilty
    but the demon
            who fills me
    with bacilli
            and you with the love of art."

                    *

        Their time-tracks met thereafter
        in supercharged sections
        rather than a long, ropy
                        taffyflow

54

Gorky and the Police Guard

In the fall of '01
Gorky ignored his travel restrictions
and stayed for a week at Chekhov's house in Yalta

> Gorky had been allowed by
> tsar-raff
> to go to the Crimea
> but was barred from staying
> in any of the Crimea's bigger cities

> Chekhov's village, Autka,
> was an unincorporated suburb of Yalta
> and thus, on a technicality,
>   Gorky could crash with Chekhov.

> And as for Yalta,
> Gorky could visit ,
>   but not stay there overnight.

A policeman stood guard at the garden gate
and the record is silent
        on whether Chekhov's pet cranes
        would shriek and waltz with joy
                at the guard
but whenever Gorky left the chief of police called Chekhov
and asked where he had gone.

> "Gorky (whom Chekhov calls Alexei Maximovich)
> is here and in good health

> He's staying at my house
>   and is officially registered here

> A policeman came by today."

Also living near Yalta
that late '01 was Leo Tolstoy

There was a gov't ban
on mentioning Tolstoy in telegrams

and because the Orthodox church
had excommunicated him

the press was prevented from
carrying news

Tolstoy was extremely well known
and the rumors on him
                wended weirdly—
that he was near death, for instance,
which wasn't true

Chekhov wrote Olga
he'd refer to Tolstoy
         as "grandpa"
when he talked about
him in telegrams to her

55

A Few From 1902

Bad health.
    His "standard remedies:"
            cod liver oil and creosote.

*

In February Olga came to Yalta
for five days of love,

and then rushed back to star
when the Art Theatre
did *Three Sisters*
for tsar Nicholas II.

Also in February
Gorky was elected honorary member
of the Imperial Academy of Sciences
(literary division),

This was during wild student disturbances
and the closing of universities
in Petersburg and Kiev

In March
secret police chief
sent Gorky's police record
to the tsar

and on March 9
the president of the Imperial Academy
was informed the tsar was pissed

at the election of a human
who was under police surveillance

March 10, the gov't ordered the Academy
to cancel the Gorky election

Throughout the spring
people wrote Chekhov
in Yalta to get involved.

∗

Olga was pregnant
and miscarried during
the season in St. Petersburg

was taken to a hospital
for an emergency operation.

She came to Yalta in April
                    carried from the steamer
                                        on a stretcher

She seemed to improve
and they went to Moscow in May

where she was badly ill again
with peritonitis.

He nursed her day and night
till she pulled well in June.

                        *

That month he visited a mine and foundries
                    in the Ural Mountains
owned by one Savva Morozov
                    a rich backer of the Moscow Art Theater

He scolded Morozov
            like a Norman Thomas Social Democrat
and persuaded him to lower
                        his workers' workday
                                    from 12 to 8.

            Idti v narod

                        *

The summer of '02

            he carried a flask
            & spat
            thrombs of blood
                        into it

                        *

208

While he was staying in the Urals
a young engineering student named Tikhonov
was assigned to attend to the writer.

He slept in the next room
& heard Chekhov wheezing & hacking
get up to pace
   drink from a glass

till finally
  the house was asleep
    in thunder and lightning and rain
when Chekhov began to groan
    with a sound like vomiting
Tikhonov ran to the room

to find him
  on his side
    in a jumble of sheets
trembling convulsively,
   his long neck over the bed edge
     coughing jerks of blood
      into a blue enamel basin.

Chekhov wiped the blood from his beard
and said softly,
  "I have disturbed your sleep
  forgive me my friend."

      *

At the end of August,
  under pressure from friends, he resigned his membership
   in the Academy of Sciences
    to protest the banning of Gorky.

A few weeks later he began *The Cherry Orchard*,
and the nudging began from his wife
   & of course from Vladimir Nemirovich-Danchenko,
who wrote him,
   "Don't read the papers.

I find that reading the press
destroys one's desire to work."

*

Body Fading
Brain Boiling

*

Striving for Bios

"I wanted to
take Hunyadi Janos
as usual,"
        he wrote to Olga
"but in Yalta
it seemed not
to be the real thing
& gave me palpitations
for two days afterward"

        and a few days later:
    "as soon as
        you learn from
        my letter or telegram
        I'm coming

        send at once
        to the chemist
        and get me
        1/2 lb
        pure refined codliver oil
        & 10 gr. of *creosoti-fagi*"

*

He wrote his elegant wife
he knew he was badly dressed

There been a bumpkinization of attire
He realized he'd lost his
big city big-time-writer
                    sartorial fluff

"My nails are long
          & there is no one
                    to snip them
In my mouth a tooth has broken
A button has dropped
                    off my
                         waistcoat."

                ✳

          Body fading
          Brain boiling

56

1903

Olga's wavering guilt that she was in Moscow
                    and her husband in Yalta.

    January 20, he wrote her: "Try and be sensible: if you lived
with me in Yalta all winter, your life would be ruined and I'd
feel pangs of conscience, which would hardly be better. I knew
I was marrying an actress, after all; what I mean is, when I
married you, I was fully aware you'd be spending winters in
Moscow. I don't feel a millionth bit hurt or cheated; on the
contrary, I think things are just fine or as they should be, so
don't bother me with your conscience anymore, sweetheart."

                ✳

Lenin in Geneva

In April, '03, Vladimir Lenin
          and his wife Krupskaya
              settled in Geneva.
He was very combative
Highly disciplined, good organizer, didn't need sleep.
Everything, every act, each dot of ink
suffused with the anxious malady
known as
        "Last Leaflet Before the Rev."

He divided the world in two:
        those with him/those against him
as he built a political structure
that looked to him for every nuance:
      the future cloth of
         the Communist Party

                *

      Lenin's Law:
      Salus revolutionis lex suprema est

                *

The Change in Images

        '82

    Tall
        broad shouldered
              a wide-brimmed black hat

    good manners
          pumping people
                for interesting anecdotes

'03

The exhausted look
Th' funereal clothing
The tattery beard
The pince-nez

⁕

However shaky and sick,
        Chekhov became an editor of *Russkaya mysl*
                (*Russian Thought*) in the late Yalta winter.
Just a short walk in his garden with his dogs
would make him sit and catch his breath.

His last story, "Betrothed" or "The Bride."
He began *The Cherry Orchard* in Feb. '03.

Visitors, such as Bunin and Gorky, would visit to cheer him up.
But he had "an indifference bordering on lethargy,"
                cane between his legs,
                        staring to the distance.

All energy: art

⁕

In the spring he escaped to Moscow,
    but it took half an hour
        huffing and heezing
            stopping every five steps

        to his third floor flat.

⁕

A friend of his wife
invited them to spend the spring
at an estate outside Moscow
        near Naro-Fominskoe

In this huge dacha he learned of
a horrible pogrom in Kishinev
in southern Russia
            with 49 killed and 500 injured

There was nothing about it in
the gov'-groveling press
In fact, the Russian gov't censored
        all telegraph messages
                from Kishinev

*

The gossip was that the pogrom was the
work of right wing nuts instigated or protected by the police

Chekhov asked Suvorin
to send him the clandestine Marxist newspaper
Liberation, in which Gorky had
        written an open letter about Kishinev.

57

The Kishinev Pogrom

On Feb 16
            '03

a young man was
murdered in a village
not far from the Bessarabian town
            of Kishinev

(the murderer later turned
out to be a relative
            wanting part of the victim's fortune)

The rumor arose

that Jews had killed
him for Christian blood in the Passover bread.

A local anti-Semitic paper, *The Bessarabetz*,
                              kept up the charge

It was the only gov't-licensed paper
                              in the area

The owner of *The Bessarabetz*, one Krushevan,
also had a paper published in St. Petersburg.

                    *

An Okhrana agent, Baron Levandel
had been sent to Kishinev to destroy
the town's burgeoning rev movement
ten months before the pogrom

and anti-semitic agitation increased
              after the Okh'-barf's arrival

                    *

According to a writer named
Michael Davitt
who spent 8 days in Kishinev
        just after the pogroms

(for a book *Within the Pale*,
  published in N.Y. in 1903)

the Chief Rabbi of Kishinev
went to the Orthodox bishop
and asked him to calm the populace
by saying no such ritual
                  was practiced

but the bishop replied
that yes he feared
some Jewish sect did exist

which used Christian blood
in the "Paschal ceremonies"

and therefore he refused to speak out.

∗

The riot-slime smashed and beat
Somehow they tore apart featherbeds and pillows,
probably looking for money

so that the streets were filled
with squalls of feathers
that eerily drifted
on thug thick streets

∗

To his eternal discredit
Suvorin's *Novoya Vremya*
repeated the hemic slander
from the right wing Kishinev press

∗

June 18, the great writer Sholem Aleichem
asked Chekhov for a story for an anthology
to benefit the victims of Kishinev.

He was too ill to write one afresh
but "Difficult People" was translated into Yiddish
for the collection published in Warsaw

58

A Few Results

On June 15, '03 the Russian gov't
abolished a few penalties

in hard labor compounds,
and in the Siberian and Sakhalin penal colonies:

- shaving of the head
- lashing
- prisoners shackled to wheel-barrows

The wheel-barrow punishment existed only on Sakhalin and
was described in Chekhov's book, and therefore
        it could be argued, that the reform
        came about through the influence
        of *The Island of Sakhalin.*

*

The Birth of the Bolsheviks

In July of '03
delegates from secret socialist groups
from all over Russia
        quietly came to Geneva
for the second congress of the
All-Russian Social Democratic Labor Party
They kept apart from one another in public
and from the Russian émigré community
        in Geneva.

The congress was adjourned to Brussels
but there were tsarist informers
and hostility from Brussels officialdom

so the congress moved,
        with 57 delegates,
                to London.

This was the congress that saw the famous split
between the Bolskeviks (Lenin's "majority")
            and the Mensheviks.

*

Lenin was very interested in the descriptions
of violent street action in Kiev:

"The time when protestors
                unfurled the Red flag, shouted
                                'Down with Absolutism!'
then fled in all directions, is over!

It is necessary to begin its *physical* destruction
                                by mass attack
The bullies of absolutism
                must receive two, or better, four blows
for each dealt out to a worker, a student, or a peasant."

✳

September 26, a telegram to Olga in Moscow:
"Four acts completely ready. Copying.
Shall send you. Health improving. Warm.
                Kiss you. Antoine."

Chekhov submitted *The Cherry Orchard*
to the censorship apparatus
for a final caress from the Nobodaddy
who banned some lines
                on worker's living conditions
                and on the lasting demoralization
                                passed on from serfdom

(Have these been restored?)

59

"To Moscow! To Moscow!"

He lived the winter of '03-'04 in Moscow
The writer Ivan Bunin spent just about
every night with Chekhov

Olga would party
and trail home late

"Every evening I visited Chekhov
and stayed with him till three or four A.M.
until Olga Leonardova came home

She usually went to the theater
or to a charity concert

Nemirovich-Danchenko would fetch her
in white tie and tails
smelling of cigars and eau-de-Cologne

She wore an evening dress,
                    beautiful, young and scented

I would kiss her hand and they would leave
Chekhov would never let me go before
                                    their return."

＊

To Ivan Bunin
dry eyes, no tears:
"I'll be forgotten in seven years."

＊

One Reason for Cigarettes

In December of '03
a right wing nut tried to stab Gorky
as he walked along the Volga at night

The knife pierced his coat and jacket
                    but was blunted
                              by Maxim's cigarette case.

＊

219

Party Time

There was a New Year's party at
           The Moscow Art Theater
                    early in '04
They feasted
      then danced

The beautiful Olga was asked to the floor
while Chekhov and Gorky
tried to talk o'er the music and party purr
Soon both were coughing
                  coughing coughing
Chekhov leaned over to
      the author of *The Lower Depths*:

"People might say of us,
'They exchanged some highly interesting coughs.'"

✳

Aeschylus—Part IV

The Cherry Orchard

Chekhov attended rehearsals,
      didn't like what they were doing to his play
& Stanislavsky didn't like Chekhov butting in.

There's a problem
when an author thinks he's written a comedy
and the director thinks its a social drama

✳

Strokes, Folks

Stanislavsky had called it
"a truly great tragedy"

Chekhov had replied,
"It is a farce."

60

1904

The Cherry Orchard premiered January 17
        his 44th birthday.
                at the Moscow Art Theater
Chekhov stayed home.
      At the end of Act 2 Stanislavsky and Nemirovich-Danchenko
        sent him a note that th' audience had been
           calling for him

He arrived at the end of Act 3,
           was hurrahed onstage,
while the audience cheered and thunder-clapped,
the author striving mightily not to cough

There were gifts and flowers in piles in front of him,
and speeches of glorification from
        journalists, actors and heads of literary societies
in a contest of quick-planned praise

There was an element in it as if he were already
                    in the grave.

It took an hour, and Chekhov could not say a word,
        but left the footlights exhausted.

✻

The Russo-Japanese War of '04

Both countries thirsted
                    to thrust into Manchuria and Korea
Japan attacked the Russian fleet
and made much death and ship-sink
                    another humiliation for Russia

about which the failing Chekhov
                    was very little attentive

"It is not the Russian people, but the Autocracy
   that has suffered shameful defeat,"
                              Lenin wrote.
"This defeat is the prologue to the
                    capitulation of Tsarism!!"

                    *

The Cherry Orchard was touring the provinces to full houses.

                    He ever more greatly
                              had trouble breathing
                    He'd quake with fever
                    Acute pains in his arms and legs

                    His doctor gave him morphine
                              shoot-ups

      yet the brain-vim
              could not be killed
      He wrote oodles of letters

      and arranged for more books to be sent
              to the Taganrog library

      and scanned and marked up manuscripts
                    for *Russkaya mysl.*
                    (*Russian Thought*)

                    *

Body Fading, Brain Boiling

Toward the end
he was glutted with visitors,

too weak to write
though he hatched new plays in his mind
and recopied in ink his notebooks

*

He told Ivan Bunin,
    "I'm going away to peg out."

Bunin thought he went
    so as not to die in front of his family.

*

On June 3rd
    with Olga by train
        to a German health resort
            at Badenweiler
                in the Black Forest

June 29 a hideous body-wracking attack,
the doctor gave him morphine and O_2

then another wracking.

He told his bank in Berlin
    to make all payments in his wife's name.

*

At the same time
Vladimir Lenin
    and his wife Krupskaya
began a month-long walk,
with knapsacks, through the Swiss countryside

Lenin was near a nervous breakdown
             from months of shrilly-dilly factionalism

and allowed the waterfalls, the blue lakes,
the glaciers: Geneva to Lausanne to Interlaken
to Lucerne
             —in the whirling patterns of Gaia
             to ease the mania.

61

At 2 AM the doctor arrived,
Chekhov covered in sweat,
and spotting the doctor
Chekhov sat up,
leaned against his pillows,
and said, "Ich sterbe."

The doctor gave him a
             camphor injection
and was sending for an
             oxygen pillow

but Chekhov said,
"What's the use?
Before it arrives
             I'll be a corpse."

In response Dr. Schwohrer
sent for champagne,
Chekhov held a glass
and said to Olga
"It's been so long since
             I've had champagne,"

and ever slowly drank it down
then lay upon his side

A black-winged moth

had come through the window
and was beating
              its wild wings
                        against the lamp.

APPENDICES

Books consulted during the creation of *Chekhov*

Chekhov, Henri Troyat. Fawcett Columbine, 1988

Anton Chekhov's Life & Thought— Selected Letters & Commentary, Simon Karlinsky (translated by Karlinsky and Michael Heim). University of California, 1975

Chekhov, Sophie Lafitte. Scribners, 1973

A Life of Chekhov, Irene Nemirovsky. London, Grey Walls Press, 1950

Chekhov, A Biography, Ernest J. Simmons. Atlantic Monthly Book, Little, Brown & Company, 1962

Chekhov—A Spirit Set Free, V.S. Pritchett. Random House, 1988

A New Life of Chekhov, Ronald Hingley. Knopf, 1976

Letters of Anton Pavlovitch Tchehov to Olga Leonardovna Knipper, translated by Constance Garnett. George Doran Co., N.Y., ca 1924

The Life and Letters of Anton Tchekhov, translated and edited by S.S. Koteliansky and Philip Tomlinson. George Doran Company, N.Y., ca 1923

Letters of Anton Chekhov, selected and edited by Avrahm Yarmolinsky. Viking, 1973

The Portable Chekhov, with intro by Avrahm Yarmolinsky. Viking, 1947

The Short Stories of Anton Chekhov, with introduction by Robert Linscott. The Modern Library, 1959

The Selected Letters of Anton Chekhov, edited and with an introduction by Lillian Hellman. Farrar, Straus & Giroux, 1955–1984

Plays. Penguin Classics edition, introduction by Elisaveta Fen, 1959

Gorky— A Biography, Henry Troyat. Crown, 1989

The Notebooks of Anton Chekhov. B. W. Huebsch, Inc. N.Y., 1922

Anton Tchekhov—Literary and Theatrical Reminiscences (Suvorin's Diary) Benjamin Blom. N.Y., 1927

Turgenev—The Man, His Art and His Age, Avrahm Yarmolinsky. The Orion Press, 1959

My Life in Art, Konstantin Stanislavsky. Routledge/Theater Arts Books, N.Y., 1994

Stanislavsky, A Life, David Magarshack. Faber and Faber, 1986

plus various editions of the stories of Anton Chekhov.

On Pre-Revolutionary Russia and Europe

Numerous entries on Russia, the Ottoman Empire, anti-Semitism, *et alia multa*, in the *Encylopedia Brittanica*, 11th Edition, 1911

The First Russian Revolution, 1825, Anatole Mazour. Stanford University Press, 1978

Russia Under the Old Regime, Richard Pipes. Scribner's, 1974

Lenin, David Shub. Penguin Books, 1967

The Evolution of Russia, Otto Hoetzsch. Harcourt, Brace and World, 1966

A Dictionary of Modern History, 1789–1945. Penguin Books, 1967

The Russian Revolution, Marcel Liebman. Vintage, 1967

The Communist Manifesto, Karl Marx and Friedrich Engels. Bantam Classic, 1992

Pushkin, Selected Verse with an introduction by John Fennell. Penguin, 1964

William Blake and the Age of Revolution, J. Bronowski. Harper & Row, 1965

The KGB, Graham Yost. Facts on File, N.Y., 1989

Revolutions of 1848, Priscilla Robertson. Harper Torchbooks, 1960

Russia's Rulers Under the Old Regime, Dominic Lieven. Yale University Press, 1990

Europe, Mother of Revolutions, Friedrich Heer. Praeger, 1972

The Revolutionary Catechism. International Workers of the World Reprint, N.Y., 1970

The Keys to Happiness—Sex and the Search for Modernity in Fin-de-Siècle Russia, Laura Engelstein. Cornell U. Press, 1992

Village Life in Late Tsarist Russia, by Olga Semyonova Tian-Shanskaia. Indiana U. Press, 1993

Hidden From History: Rediscovering Women in History from the 17th Century to the Present, Sheila Rowbotham. Random House, 1974 (Chapter, "Birth Control and Early Nineteenth Century Radicalism")

Sex & Destiny: The Politics of Human Fertility, Germaine Greer. Harper Colophon, 1985 (Chapter, "The Short History of Contraception")

The Nature of Russia, John Massey Stewart. Boxtree Ltd., London, 1992

Muzhik and Muscovite, Joseph Bradley, University of California Press, 1985

On Pogroms and Anti-Semitism in Russia

Cops & Rebels— A Study of Provocation, Paul Chevigny. Pantheon, 1972

World of Our Fathers, Irving Howe. Schocken Books, 1989

The Voice of America on Kishineff, edited by Cyrus Adler. The Jewish Publication Society of America, 1904

Easter in Kishinev—Anatomy of a Pogrom, Edward H. Judge. New York University Press, 1992

Troubled Waters—The Origins of the 1881 Anti-Jewish Pogroms in Russia, I. Michael Aronson. University of Pittsburgh, 1990

Within the Pale—The True Story of Anti-Semitic Persecutions in Russia, Michael Davitt. A. S. Barnes & Co, N.Y., 1903

The Jews in Russia, Volume I, The Struggle for Emancipation, Louis Greenberg. Yale University Press, 1944

The Russian Jew Under Tsars and Soviets, Salo W. Baron. Macmillan, N.Y.

Zola & the Dreyfus Case. Gordon Press, N.Y., 1972

Agents of Deceit: Frauds, Forgeries and Political Intrigue Among Nations, Paul W. Blackstock. Quadrangle Books, Chicago, 1966

231

On the Writing of *Chekhov*

When I came to New York City in the late '50s, the first play I saw was *Ivanov*. In the '60s when I opened the Peace Eye Bookstore in the Lower East Side, I stocked as many of Chekhov's books as I could find, and began to read his short stories. "Rothschild's Fiddle," "The Grasshopper," and "In the Ravine" were among my favorites.

When my family moved to Woodstock in '74, I discovered the local library had the 13-volume collection of Constant Garnett's translations of Chekhov, which that year I read in its entirety.

After moving to Woodstock, I began writing musicals, among which were "The Karen Silkwood Cantata" and "Star Peace," and I made plans to write a musical drama based on Chekhov's 1884 tale, "Rothschild's Fiddle." Unfortunately I have not yet completed the "Rothschild's Fiddle" project, although I still think it would make a fine one- or two-act piece.

In 1985 I was in Baton Rouge, Louisiana for a literary festival and I visited the painter Alice Codrescu, who showed me her painting "Chekhov and Gorky." The images of Gorky and Chekhov in her painting stayed with me, so a few years later, in 1990, I began a poem called "The Paintings of Chekhov," in which I urged Alice to paint other scenes from Chekhov's life, such as the incidents in which he had built schools or organized famine relief or provided free medical care in rural areas.

Later, in '91, I made notes for a "Hymn to Chekhov," an investigative poem in the tradition of extended works I had written such as "Melville's Father," "Hymn to Archilochus," "Yiddish Speaking Socialists of the Lower East Side," and a long poem I was working on at the time, "Cassandra."

In 1992 and 1993 I was very occupied in the writing and staging of a musical drama, *Cassandra*, on the life of the ancient Trojan prophetess. There was a production in Woodstock in the late summer of '93 during which time I began thinking about writing another musical drama and was just about to commit to a musical on the life of Sappho.

One evening while I was driving to the theater for a performance of *Cassandra* the word "Chekhov" came into my mind.

Yes! I thought, why not do a musical drama on his life that would also feature some of the history and political movements in Russia in the late 19th/early 20th century?

In the fall of '93 I started research on Chekhov's life in libraries, and began work on song ideas, dialogue and characters. I decided to assemble a detailed chronology on his life and times. The material on Chekhov is very extensive, even in English, and it didn't take much reading to realize just how complicated and interesting his life and milieu were. There was so much material that I was bewildered as to how to translate these gluts of particulars into a play.

It was then, after I had assembled a tentative chronology, that I decided to write a poem on his life and times. It seemed apparent that the method I had developed for writing *Cassandra* would work for creating a musical drama on the life of Chekhov. For *Cassandra* I created a 26-page poem that served as the treatment for the drama. The poem "Cassandra" was published in my collection, *Hymn to the Rebel Cafe*.

My hope was that, as in the case of *Cassandra*, out of the poem's text would come ideas for songs, dramatic vignette, narrator, chorus and structure for the drama. When I began, I thought the poem on Chekhov might be thirty or forty pages long.

I worked every day on *Chekhov* for six months till completing a draft in early 1994. I read sections from it at performances throughout the year, testing its strength. Then there was additional research, visiting libraries and gathering books from stores and the lists and catalogues of book dealers, during which time I reworked the poem and finished it in the late fall.

The biography of a genius like Chekhov is somewhat like an anthology of great poetry. One selects and sequences what seems the very best, but realize that other minds might select and sequence somewhat differently.

Of course, I owe a great debt to the scholarship of others. There are a number of wonderful books on Chekhov and his era, many of which are listed in the Appendix.

It was my training as a bard—reading poetry and living poetry and writing poetry almost every day for forty years that prepared me to create *Chekhov*. Never had I experienced such fun in a long writing project as during the months of Chekhov. I found myself swept up in his vitality, his creativity and his burning desire to enmesh himself in his era. It was a time of joy for me to bring my studies in meter, my musical training, my sense of visuality and line break, and my theoretical work on "Investigative Poetry" to such a challenging project.

It was apparent as I began to mix and arrange the flow of information that a verse biography of Chekhov could extend to five or ten thousand pages. That was part of the fun, the thrill of choosing with bardic mind the meters, the line breaks, the "data clusters," the vignettes, the historical data, the selections from letters and memoirs, to form the sequences of vowels, consonants and syllables that in their thousandfold array give life to this poem on Chekhov.

And now, hopefully, I will be able to create from *Chekhov* a musical drama on his life.

One thing that occurred to me during the research is that there may be considerable additional material—notes, diaries, letters, and maybe even manuscripts that have been held back by the Soviets and by his family. I wonder if parts of the novel he was working on in 1889, *Stories from the Lives of My Friends*, which he abandoned in good part because he feared the censors would never allow its publication, may still exist. There may also be additional letters of Chekhov in the unshared archives of friends and associates which in the post-Soviet era could safely be published. No doubt Chekhov scholars are already examining these possibilities.

I am very, very grateful to John Martin and the staff at Black Sparrow Press for publishing this study of the life and times of a very great writer, Anton Pavlovich Chekhov.

Edward Sanders
Woodstock, New York

A Chronology of Many of
the Works of Anton Chekhov

1878   Sample juvenilia:
Why the Hen Clucked, a farce (lost)
He's Met His Match, a satirical comedy (lost)

1879 (Dec 24) First ink: "A Letter from a Don Squire Stepan
Vladimirovich N. to His Learned Neighbor
Doctor Friedrich," published in *Strekoza* (The
Dragonfly)

1881   *Platonov,* a four-act play, destroyed, but early draft later
found in Chekhov's archives
"St. Peter's Day"

1880–1884 Wrote around 300 humorous pieces for mags under
an assortment of noms de ha-ha, among them:
"Things Most Frequently Encountered in Novels, Stories
and Other Such Things"
"Appropriate Measures"
"Surgery"
"The Medal"
"Promotion by Examination"
"A Horsey Name"
"The Lady of the Manor"
"For Little Apples"

1882   Serialized satirical novel, *A Useless Victory,* in 8 parts.
"The Late-Blooming Flowers"

1883   "The Portrait" (unpublished story rejected by *Strekosa,*
'83)
"Intercession"
"Rapture"
"The Death of a Civil Servant" or "The Death of an
Official"
"The Daughter of Albion"
"Fat and Thin"
"An Enigmatic Character"

"The Only Remedy"
"Thief" ("The Culprit"?)
"Willow"
"Fragments of Moscow Life" (monthly column in
    Fragments)

1884   *Melpomene* A collection of humorous tales by Antosha
            Tchekhonté
        The Shooting Party, unpublished murder mystery
        "The Corpse"
        "Vacation Rules and Regulations"
        "Oysters"
        "A Dreadful Night"
        "The Complaints Book"
        "Rothschild's Fiddle"
        "The Chameleon"

1885   Chekhov published 129 stories and sketches, including:
        "The Criminal" or "The Malefactor"
        "The Huntsman"
        "The Requiem"
        "A Man of Ideas"
        "Sadness" ("The Misfortune"?)
        "Sgt. Prishibeyev"

1886   Chekhov 112 stories and sketches, including:
        "Agafya"
        "Other People's Misfortune"
        "Romance with Double Bass"
        "Dreams"
        "Grisha"
        "Good People"
        "Kids"
        "Revenge"
        "Easter Night"
        "The Witch"
        "The Objet d'Art"
        "Heartache"
        "The Requiem"
        "The Chorus Girl"

"Mire"
"On the Road"
"Anyuta"
"A Calamity"
"Vanka"
"The Orator"
"The Privy Councilor"
  Motley Tales or *Varicolored Stories*, 375 page collection
  The Swan Song one act play
"For the Information of Husbands"—nearly totally cut
    by censors
  On the High Road, a play banned by censor

1887   66 stories and sketches (he's writing fewer and better),
          including:
"The Mystery"
"A Cossack" (April)
"Typhus"
"A Drama"
"The Beggar"
"The Kiss"
"The Siren"
"An Encounter"
"The Letter"
"The Weariness of Life"
"Verochka"
"Notes from the Journal of a Quick-Tempered Man"
"The Reed Pipe"
  At Twilight a collection of stories
  Ivanov, a play in four acts
  Innocent Talk (or *Innocent Words*), a collection of stories

1888   12 stories, including:
"The Steppe"
"Sleepy"
"Lights"
"The Birthday Party" or "The Name-Day Party"
"The Belles"
"Nervous Breakdown" or "An Attack of Nerves"
"The Fit"

"An Unpleasantness"
"First-Class Passenger"
"The Gardener and the Evil Spirit"
"No Comment"
"Let Me Sleep"
The Bear, a one act farce
"Moscow Hypocrites" unsigned editorial in *Novoya Vremya*
"In Praise of Explorers"   "   "   "   "   "
Stories, a collection of nine tales

1889   *The Wood Demon*, a comedy in four acts
        "A Tedious Story" or "A Dreary Story"
        The Proposal, a one act farce
        The Forced Declaration, an anonymous brief skit
        Morose People or *Gloomy People*

1890   *A Tragedian Against His Will*, a one act farce
        "The Demons" or "The Thieves"
        "Gusev"
        "Champagne"
        "Siberian Notes," series of articles in *Novoya Vremya* in
            the summer.

1891   "The Duel"
        "Women"
        "Kashtanka" (childrens story)

1892   "Ward Number 6"
        "The Grasshopper"
        "The Wife" or "My Wife" (summer)
        "In Exile"
        "The Neighbors"
        "The Duel"
        "My Patient's Story"

1893   "The Chorus Girl"
        "The Story of an Unknown Man"
        "Big Volodya and Little Volodya"
        Sakhalin Island: Notes of a Journey (serialized in *Russkaia
            Mysl*)

238

1894 "The Black Monk"
      "A Woman's Kingdom"
      "The Story of the Head Gardener"
      Tales and Stories

1895 "The House with the Mezzarine (Mansard?)"
      The Island of Sakhalin: Travel Notes (as a book)
      The Seagull, a comedy in four acts (first version)
      "Three Years"
      "The Murder"
      "Ariadne"
      "The Wife"
      "Anna on the Neck"
      "White Brow" (children's story)

1896 "My Life"
      The Seagull (second version)

1897 "Peasants"
      "In a Native Spot"
      "In the Cart"
      "The Homecoming" ("At Home"?)
      "The Pecheneg"

1898 *Uncle Vanya*, scenes from country life in four acts
      "A Man in a Case" or "The Man in a Shell"
      "A Visit with Friends"
      "Ionych"
      "The Lodger"
      "The Husband"
      "The Darling"
      "Gooseberries"
      "On Love" or "About Love"
      "The New Villa" (late in year)

1899 "The Lady with a Dog"
      "The New Bungalow"
      "On Official Business"
      "The Darling"
      "In the Ravine"

1900   *Three Sisters*, a drama in four acts
        "At Christmas Time"
1901   "Women"

1902   "The Bishop"
        "A Letter"—unfinished story

1903   "The Bride" (Feb.)
        The Cherry Orchard, a comedy in four acts

Printed March 1995 in Santa Barbara
& Ann Arbor for the Black Sparrow Press by
Mackintosh Typography & Edwards Brothers Inc.
Text set in Monotype Book Antiqua by Words Worth.
Design by Barbara Martin.
This edition is published in paper wrappers;
there are 200 hardcover trade copies;
100 hardcover copies have been numbered & signed
by the author; & 26 copies handbound in boards
by Earle Gray are lettered & signed by the author.

Photo: Miriam Sanders

EDWARD SANDERS was born in Kansas City, Missouri in 1939, and attended Blue Springs High School, a few miles from Harry Truman's house. After graduating from New York University in 1964 with a degree in Classics, he founded the legendary Peace Eye Book Store in New York's Lower East Side and the folk rock group the Fugs. The Fugs created eleven albums during their career, a number of which are still in print.

Sanders was active in the Social Democratic wing of the counterculture of the 1960s and '70s and published a number of influential magazines and manifestoes.

For the last eighteen years he has been active in the environmental, peace, economic justice and consumer movements in Woodstock, New York, where he lives, during which time he has written books of verse, poetics, novels, collections of short stories and works of nonfiction.

His collected poems, 1961–1985, *Thirsting for Peace in a Raging Century*, won an American Book Award in 1988. The updated edition of *The Family*, his study of the Manson group, was published in 1990. *Tales of Beatnik Glory, Volumes I and II* (1990) is being made into a feature-length film.

His musical drama *Cassandra*, based on texts from Euripides, Aeschylus, Apollodorus and Homer, had its premiere performances in 1992. Sanders' *Songs in Ancient Greek* (1992) is available on compact disk.

He is at work on Volume III of *Tales of Beatnik Glory, Tuxedo by Water*, a true crime story, and a book of poetics, *Investigative Poetry and Beyond*. His most recent book of poetry, *Hymn to the Rebel Cafe*, was published by Black Sparrow in 1993.